T3-BOE-374

The Newspaper in the American Novel 1900-1969

by

Thomas Elliott Berry

The Scarecrow Press, Inc.
Metuchen, N. J. 1970

ISBN 0-8108-0334-8

Preface

This book, as the title indicates, discusses the portrayal of the Twentieth Century American newspaper in the American novel. Therefore, the book is essentially a discussion of the attempts of American novelists within this period to interpret one or more phases of American newspaper journalism.

The entire work is based on two premises. First, it rests on the conviction that the complex nature and the far-reaching significance of the American newspaper can be explained only by a competent interpretation of the total institution of American newspaper journalism. Second, it arises from the concept that because the novelist's interpretations of institutions often exert a strong impact on the conclusions held by society, the interpretations of the American newspaper by American novelists merit a careful examination.

In preparing this book, the author has considered all the American novels of this period that touch any phase of the American newspaper. In addition, however, he has examined all the works of the major novelists of the time--whether or not they depict any aspect of the newspaper--in order to assess wherever possible the particular novelist's view of American journalism. The reasoning is that both the history of American literature and the history of American newspaper journalism can be enriched by learning the attitude of our major novelists toward our newspapers.

For convenience of treatment, the work is divided into six chapters. The first serves to present the pertinent background material for understanding the Twentieth Century

American newspaper. The succeeding three chapters then handle the portrayal of the newspaper in the American novel by separating the sixty-nine year span into three periods: 1900-30, 1930-50, and 1950-69. The fifth chapter is a separate consideration of the individual newspaperman as depicted in novels throughout the total period. An entire chapter is devoted to the working journalist because of his central position in the vast newspaper scene. To close the book, a short conclusion is presented.

Naturally, the author of a book of this kind must rely on many others for assistance. Although thanking everyone meriting recognition is impossible, the author must acknowledge the many newspapermen and fellow teachers of American literature who read parts or all of the manuscript and made valuable suggestions.

T. E. B.

West Chester, Pennsylvania

Contents

Chapter 1

The Twentieth Century American Newspaper

The newspaper in the United States is unquestionably one of the most significant institutions within our national culture. Currently, 1,534 papers are printed daily with a total circulation of 60,381,142, while 556 are printed on Sundays with a total circulation of 49,230,487.[1] In addition, the results of a nationwide study conducted by Audits and Survey Company[2] show that 80.5 percent of our nation's men and 79 percent of our nation's women peruse a newspaper every day, while 88 percent of American adults read at least one newspaper on one or more days of every five-day period. Hence, the extent of newspaper readership is an impressive fact within our pattern of living.

However, although readership statistics clearly establish the strong place of the newspaper in our national life, they reveal little of the final nature of the newspaper's influence on our citizenry. This influence--which has long been scrutinized with varying degrees of intensity by observers of social, political and other behavioral patterns--is known to exert itself in every area of contemporary thought. It is also known to be one of the most powerful determinants in many conclusions held by society in general.

The difficulty of delineating this influence lies in first isolating the influence itself for proper study and analysis. Sometimes, of course, a particular influence can be seen quite clearly. The great number of persons, high and low, who rely on leading newspapers for guidance in interpreting foreign affairs represents an obvious influence of the newspaper. Similarly, the many persons who quote approvingly a widely known columnist indicate an obvious influence, as do the thousands who extract information from newspapers for use in teaching and similar undertakings. On the other hand, the influence of the newspaper can be a subtle or even a baffling matter. Who can describe the exact strength of newspaper influence in molding popular opinion on crime and divorce? Who can chart accurately the force of newspaper advertising in extending the use of tobacco and intoxicating liquor? Who can evaluate the power of the gossip columnist in encouraging readers to snoop into other people's business, or the weight of a particular comic strip in shaping the values of children? Without doubt, an influence exists in each of these instances, but any analysis of the influence must be largely conjectural.

(On occasions, incidents involving the influence of the newspaper have presented some interesting sidelights on American history. President Franklin D. Roosevelt often cited jubilantly his overwhelming success at the polls in the face of the opposition of the majority of the nation's newspapers. President Harry S. Truman never let many prominent newspapers forget that they had advocated and predicted his defeat by Governor Thomas E. Dewey. President John F. Kennedy undoubtedly received the margin of votes necessary for his narrow victory through the support of the nation's newspaper writers--though not the newspaper publishers. President Lyndon B. Johnson was glaringly unsuccessful in his attempts to alter the newspaper-created image of a wily politician pretending to be a statesman. President Richard M. Nixon, in his first days in office, worked openly to eradicate old antipathies with newspapermen.)

The nature and degree of the newspaper's influence has been determined, until recently, principally by accepting the majority opinion of competent observers. Because national political observers, for example, agree that the editorial voices of the New York Times, the Christian Science Monitor, and the St. Louis Post-Dispatch have a strong bearing on national elections, the fact has been considered proven. Also, the fact that readers on the lower educational levels tend to be the greatest purchasers of the tabloid has been interpreted as an inter-active situation: the tabloid presents to the readers the material they desire, and they, in turn, are influenced toward remaining on a low cultural level through exposure to that same material.

Within the past three decades, however, the influence of the newspaper has been subjected to a more scientific type of analysis than heretofore. The large schools of journalism and many psychologists and others involved in the behavioral sciences have developed more exact techniques for measuring this influence and for evaluating reader reactions in general. From these studies, some interesting conclusions have emerged. Among the most important is the fact that approximately ninety-five percent of our citizenry derive ninety-eight percent of their conclusions on foreign affairs and major domestic matters from material presented by the principal media of mass communication (newspapers, magazines, radio, television). Naturally, the role of each medium cannot be separated from the others but, at the least, the newspaper can be seen as a powerful agent within this area.

Because of the highly important place of the newspaper in twentieth century life, students and critics of American civilization have frequently raised their voices in approval or protest. Clergymen have denounced specific newspapers from the pulpit; political figures have ranted against the weight of the newspaper in guiding public opinion; parent-teacher groups have protested the inclusion of certain comic strips; and many others have expressed opinions in varying degrees of strength.

As history shows, however, only those persons possessed of the insight, the powers of analysis, and the overall grasp of facts characteristic of the best of literary artists are really capable of comprehending the institutions within society. Thus a moral code is understood only by a Nathaniel Hawthorne, a social milieu only by a Henry James, and a cultural entity only by a Willa Cather. In fact, one can safely state that most of the soundest analyses of society and its problems made within the past century or more have been done by novelists. Tolstoy and Dostoevsky in Russia, Balzac and Flaubert in France, Thackeray and Dickens in England, and James and Twain in the United States are all examples of this special competence.

Because most twentieth century American novelists have been concerned at some time in their careers with major institutions within our culture, one might reasonably expect them to bring the newspaper under an intense and all-pervading scrutiny--if for no other reason, because of the influence which it exerts on our culture. Yet, as this book attempts to demonstrate, American novelists of this century have not acted according to expectation. They have examined with genuine capability many institutions within our culture--but the newspaper has not been one of them. Many novels deal with newspapers, and many with newspapermen, but the penetrating analysis and all-inclusive treatment that one would expect has never materialized.

To understand this situation, one needs first to examine the nature of the newspaper of this century; to learn something of its characteristics, its function, and its general place in the American scene.

II

Understanding the nature of the American newspaper of this century begins with the grasp of a fundamental truth: even though the newspaper of this century has always concentrated on its primary function of presenting news, it has, nonetheless, experienced some far-reaching changes in its character. Hence, when one thinks of the newspaper of this period, he must think in terms of sub-divisions within the total history of the time; he must not think of the newspaper as an unchanging institution amidst unchanging circumstances.

At the opening of the century, the newspaper was a rather simple publication which usually appeared in the large cities in three daily editions and in the rural areas in just one edition. Generally, most pages were quite black, relieved only by an occasional portrait-type picture. The action shots, the illustrative material, and the kind of advertisement now viewed as commonplace were missing; and the multi-color page and other features made possible by later mechanical advances were, of course, non-existent also.

The basic intent of this paper was to provide "news," accompanied by follow-ups and in-depth treatments of older stories. The scoop was considered highly important, especially as a means of competing with other newspapers, and every effort was made to give a hot-off-the-griddle aspect to everything except the feature material (editorials, essays, etc.) intended for later leisurely reading. In essence, this newspaper was the one source of "news" as well as the basic reading matter for almost every literate family; and it provided the great bulk of topics of conversation for the majority of people.

During the first two decades of the twentieth century, the newspaper remained in this relatively static position. Although startling improvements were made in the linotype machine, the printing press, and other related equipment; although the teletype machine and other methods of transmitting news rapidly came into being; and although feature material offerings (comics, syndicated material, etc.) greatly changed the content of the paper, the newspaper still retained its essential character as a publication designed primarily to provide information concerning that which was "new."

With the advent of the 1920's, however, there arose a new and powerful influence on the role of the newspaper: radio entered the American home as a potent competitor of the newspaper. Where formerly the newspaper had been the sole means by which the citizenry could learn quickly of major developments (Presidential appointments, earthquakes, murders, etc.), the radio now seized this function. When, for instance, President Theodore Roosevelt died on January 6, 1919, the nation at large received the news through the newspaper. But when President Warren G. Harding died on August 2, 1923, a scant four and one half years later, the nation as a whole learned of the death by radio broadcast.[3]

Because radio, from its earliest days, obviously had an unbeatable time advantage in breaking news, the newspaper felt the first sting of the competition that eventually developed into a four-way battle for the attention of the public--the competition of newspaper, magazine, radio, and television.

As a result of this first clash of newspaper and radio, the whole character of the newspaper was affected: through the rise of the "news program" of the radio, the newspaper lost the impact of surprise which it had exerted so strenuously, especially on page one, an impact upon which it had relied heavily for its great appeal.

To compensate for this lost advantage, the newspaper began to resort to in-depth coverage not possible on radio and to a more extensive use of pictures and other material not adaptable to radio broadcast. In short, it began to move into the province of the magazine, thereby forcing the magazine to fight for readers against a new form of competition. Some magazines were to be driven further into a corner in the late 1930's with the improvements in cameras that provide the excellent action shots and the clarity of detail that have brought on photojournalism (defined broadly as the reliance upon pictures rather than words to recount news, e.g., the pictorial sequence, the "news of the week in pictures," etc.) and the remarkable Sunday supplement magazines.

The early competition of newspaper and radio was eventually resolved by each striving to excel in the area wherein it held the advantage, while it shared the remaining ground with the foe. Thus the newspaper began to capitalize upon every advantage inherent in the printed page (in-depth coverage, attractive make-up, pictures, maps, etc.) while the radio increased its use of newscasts and flashes within normally scheduled programs. Meanwhile, each continued its use of interviews, feature story material, and light entertainment (jokes, quips, etc.).

This stand-off continued until the middle of the 1940's when television emerged--as had been predicted before World

War II--to compete with both the newspaper and radio. Television had a distinct advantage in its use of pictures, visual aids, live interviews, and similar devices. But it was also limited by the fact that, like radio, it could provide little selectivity for its audience and no permanent record; that is to say, many people still preferred the newspaper for news because they could select the material they wished to read, they could read at will, and they could skip and reread as they pleased. Perhaps even more important, they could save the newspaper or selected material from it as a permanent record. In looking at television, of course, they had to follow a program controlled completely by outside forces, to say nothing of offensive and time-consuming commercials.

Today, the newspaper, radio, and television have all found their place in the scheme of things. Radio, for example, is a popular medium of entertainment and information for the person who is working in the home or driving his car; television has a distinct place as family entertainment; and the newspaper, despite the increased competition, continues successfully to fill its traditional role in our national life. A word should be said in passing, however, on the effect of this four-way competition on the magazine.

The competition of the magazine against the other media has always been conducted on a relatively narrow front; that is to say, where the newspaper, radio, and television strive for the attention of a wide segment of the public, each magazine, generally speaking, focuses its attention on a fairly specific group. To illustrate, _TV Guide_ directs itself squarely at the television viewer; _Saturday Review_ points toward the well educated, intellectual group;

and Atlantic Monthly seeks the reader interested in questions of major import. The scholarly journals and the professional magazines are mostly geared to even more limited segments of the public. As a result of this situation, the competition between the magazine and the other media is basically a case of individual magazines fighting for a specific type of reader rather than one of an entire medium (the magazine) competing on a broad front against the other media (newspaper, radio, television).

A further point should be noted: the magazine (scholarly journals and similar publications excepted) is primarily interested in advertisers. Editorial content and promotional efforts are directed toward obtaining readers to use as inducements to gain advertisers. The formula of the magazine in most instances is to try to corner a section of the reading public (e.g., Seventeen and the late-teenage girl, Ebony and the Negro, Fortune and the business community) and then to sell advertising to those who desire to reach the particular group. The competition of the magazine versus the other media thus becomes fundamentally a competition for advertising accounts.

The newspaper's trend toward in-depth coverage that began with the advent of radio accelerated sharply the use of the signed column, especially those written by syndicated columnists. From the first, these columnists became, in effect, voices within a voice; that is to say, they have always been viewed as individuals apart from the newspaper in which their writings appear. The most influential of the serious columnists in the period under study (1900 to the present) has been Walter Lippmann.[4] The most outstanding humorist has been Will Rogers. The most successful writer of chit-chat has been Walter Winchell.

To say that the writers mentioned above--and the approximately fifty other columnists whose range has been only slightly less wide--have been a strong influence on the course of American journalism and on American thought in general would be to state the minimum. Each, in his particular way, has left his mark on his and later times; and each has been followed by a host of imitators who have made their power felt. Also, because of the overall appeal of the signed column, many syndicates have induced persons in other fields (federal government, entertainment, sports, etc.) to produce regular columns.

Although the emergence of the columnist was an important development in journalism, one should note that the dominant single personality had existed before, as for example, William Allen White of the Emporia Gazette and H. L. Mencken of the Paltimore Sun papers. The significance of the rise of the columnist is that it created many new individual personalities. One should note also that the emergence of many columnists of national stature has not been entirely a blessing. Some of these newly established voices have been neither great thinkers nor forces for the improvement of society. Some have been, purely and simply, limited men with an eye on personal gain, and they have been too ready to launch out on topics beyond their grasp, with little or no cognizance of the responsibility of their position as influential writers.

III

Concurrent with the impact on the newspaper of the four-way competition of newspaper, magazine, radio and television, changes in the world of business were also working an effect. The greatest influence can be summarized pointedly: with the growing industrialism, the operation of a newspaper was itself becoming, in every sense of the term, "big business." Formerly, a man could launch a paper with only a small building, a linotype machine, a press, and the bare essentials of a composing room. As circulation increased, he could then buy additional equipment and expand his plant, staff, and coverage. Now, however, starting a newspaper demanded a genuinely sizable investment. The initial equipment necessary for competition had reached prohibitive heights for the small entrepreneur, and all in all, a new era in creating newspapers had arrived.[1]

This change, in turn, produced several other important results. Most noticeable was that the old spirit of independence which often characterized the launching of a newspaper now had to be tempered with big business considerations. Thus something was lost in the realm of free and unrestricted expression. Also, the small rural papers began to dwindle because of their inability to compete with the large metropolitan papers that began to circulate, more and more, in the rural areas where they offered the reader more for his purchase price. This competition eventually became definitely one-sided as the metropolitan papers inaugurated the use of the "suburban section," thereby giving the rural and suburban dwellers two newspapers for the price of one. By far the most serious situation, however, was the growth of "mergers" and with it, the disappearance of many prominent and highly respected papers.

IV

The changing nature of the newspaper in the twentieth

century raises several questions deserving careful examination. These questions, although of the newspaper world, are actually problems of all society because of their far-reaching implications. Hence critics of society--and especially those novelists who consider themselves critics of society--must handle these problems in an attempt to find answers.

The most serious of these problems concern (1) freedom of expression, (2) attempts to establish external controls on the newspaper, and (3) chain ownership.

The question of freedom of expression revolves about a conflict of interests. The newspaper has always sought to print whatever material it may choose, in whatever manner it may see fit, without fear of repercussion from any outside force; or stated more simply, it has always claimed the right to be its own judge and censor. On the other hand, some persons or groups, for clear or obscure reasons, have wanted certain news colored or suppressed; they feel that the newspaper should handle news in terms of specific guidelines acceptable to them. As a result, a round of head-on clashes has occurred during the twentieth century, especially between the Federal Government and individual newspapers.

The first important contest occurred in 1908 when President Theodore Roosevelt had the New York World indicted in Federal Court in Washington for disclosing the means by which the United States had acquired territorial rights for the Panama Canal. Although the case made little progress, the advocates of free speech naturally were aroused; and the Nation's newspapers, as they always seem to do in such instances, rallied to the support of the World.

The next significant issue arose during World War I

when the dissemination of news was throttled vigorously by the Office of War Information under George Creel. It was clear that some news was being withheld and other news censored, but newsmen gained nothing from their vigorous protests. Also during World War I, the Post Office, of all departments, suddenly cast itself as a censoring agency. Basing its actions on provisions of the Trading with the Enemy Act (October 6, 1917), the Sedition Act (May 16, 1918), and other legislation, postal officials refused to process publications which they considered dangerous to the national welfare, indecent, or otherwise objectionable. All in all, 75 publications collided with the Post Office in one form or another, with the Post Office emerging partially or completely victorious in every instance. The futility of the protests is evident in the fact that, as of this writing, the Post Office still holds its position of censor.[6]

Even more important, however, is the fact that such terms as "anti-American," "obscene,"[7] and "objectionable" are not clearly defined by our courts. Yet the Post Office exerts a finality of judgment in applying these terms.[8]

The period immediately following World War I was relatively free of conflict in the field of freedom of expression; yet one must not conclude that the practices of the present were in vogue at that time. The newspapers have made considerable progress since that time in obtaining information from the Federal Government. In the 1920's, for example, the now familiar press conferences of the President of the United States and the Washington correspondents, with all their banter and give and take, were unknown. Press conferences were far less frequent and much more formal, and both President Coolidge and President Hoover insisted on written questions submitted in advance. The press conference as we now know it arose with President Franklin D. Roosevelt, and later the television press conference (which newspapermen as a whole dislike because of its "canned" atmosphere) developed under President Eisenhower.

Because the current type of informal press conference places the President of the United States and lesser officials in the role of defendants facing the impromptu questioning of the newspapermen, it represents a distinct step forward in freedom of expression.[9] Many newspapermen contend, with some justification, that this kind of conference is a safeguard of a democratic government; and any President would face genuine difficulty if he were now to attempt to discard the practice.

In the 1930's, the newspaper faced its most vigorous challenge--and indeed one of the most vigorous challenges of all time--during the first term of President Roosevelt. For the first year or more of his tenure, Roosevelt held a sway over Congress which occasioned the expression "Rubber Stamp Congress." Among other legislation passed almost automatically at the President's request was the historically important "National Industrial Recovery Act," an act designed to improve the Nation's troubled economy by regulating labor conditions generally. The act provided for each industry to draw up a voluntary code of fair practices which would, in effect, guarantee a minimum wage, a minimum work week, and other conditions likely to spark the sluggish economy. However, although the key word was "voluntary," the act contained some strong provisions. Among other stipulations, the act empowered the President to license any business which did not comply with a voluntary code. (Signed into law in June, 1933, the Act was ruled unconstitutional by the Supreme Court in May, 1935.)

As this provision obviously gave the President a potential control over newspapers, radio stations, and other businesses within and without the field of mass communications, pointed questions were asked of Roosevelt. These he attempted to turn aside, to answer in a light manner, or to handle with an off-hand vagueness. Many newspapers, as a result, warned Roosevelt editorially concerning the tradition of a free press in the United States; and the American Newspaper Publishers Association, in composing the Code for the industry, insisted on inserting a provision reaffirming the constitutional guarantee of freedom of the press. This latter action was prompted in part, incidentally, by the strong protests of official Washington that it was not necessary.

From World War II to the present, the most important clashes between the newspaper and the Federal government have turned on the practice of withholding news in the name of "national interest." For example, President Eisenhower's Secretary of State, John Foster Dulles, refused to grant visas to journalists desiring to visit Red China. Such visits, he ruled, were inimical to "our national interests." Despite the vigorous protests of the newspapers, Eisenhower refused to overrule Dulles, thereby seriously curbing freedom of expression in one area. The significance of this incident, of course, is that the Federal government restricted the activities of American newsmen in a nation with which our government was not at war.[10]

The administration of President John F. Kennedy was

uneventful in the area of freedom of expression. The only serious charge was that of "managed news"--which as the expression implies, is regulating the timing and content of news releases in order to benefit the administration.[11] The term "managed news" was also cast at the Lyndon B. Johnson administration--along with the phrase "credibility gap" (i.e., lack of complete veracity in fact and presentation).

As of this writing, the most serious difficulty arising between the administration of President Richard M. Nixon and the press has resulted from a series of speeches delivered by Vice President Spiro T. Agnew in October and November, 1969. Agnew, addressing receptive audiences in large Eastern cities, rebuked both television and the newspaper for "one-sided" coverage and interpretation of news. He argued in strong language that prominent television newscasters were being programmed to follow the President after an important address in order to "criticize adversely"; and he lambasted the newspapers for gaining captive audiences through "monopolistic practices."

Actually, Agnew presented no new evidence. Knowledgeable people had long been concerned about the increase in one-newspaper cities; the growth of newspaper chains; and the ownership of other media (e.g., television stations) by newspaper publishers. Agnew was merely a new drummer behind an old drum.

The Vice President's speeches also suffered from loose charges and questionable deductions. (The charges of unfair practices, for instance, which he leveled against the _New York Times_ and the _Washington Post_ were fallacious.) Furthermore, as publishers were quick to note, Agnew offered no remedy. He merely asked vaguely for some form of control while denying any desire to "censor" or "inhibit freedom of expression."

The most disturbing aspect of the Agnew attacks was the implication of Presidential approval. Although Nixon and Agnew strove to picture the Vice President as an individual speaking his own mind, few persons could accept that conclusion.

The attempts to apply external controls to the newspaper of this century have assumed two forms: those of organized groups and those of individuals. Of the attempts of organized groups, the most serious has been that of the bar associations. The majority of lawyers and judges, it seems, are seriously concerned with the oft-stated question of a "free press versus a fair trial." They argue that the media of mass communication create a prejudicial effect by presenting information about the case before it reaches court; and they further argue that any editorial judgment expressed before the actual trial is certain to influence the opinions of some prospective jurors.

Currently, majority opinion within the field of mass communication is that a defendant cannot receive a fair trial under the glare of the television camera; hence the place of television in the courtroom must be restricted.[12] However, this same majority opinion holds that some pictures of the actual trial must be permitted for newspapers and television newscasters, despite the opposition of most judges.

Much more serious is the settled conviction of newspapermen and other knowledgeable persons that any curb on the reporter, within or outside the courtroom, poses a genuine threat to our democratic system of government. They argue that with any restriction on free speech there goes an accompanying opportunity for someone--a judge, lawyer, public official, or other person--to proceed illegally. The newspaper's unrestricted right to print the truth, they argue quite cogently, is one of the strongest guarantees against the type of action that threatens our democratic form of government.

The demands of the bar associations have recently gained some reinforcement from the United States Supreme Court. In June, 1966, that court ruled by a vote of 8-1 that the State of Ohio must either free Dr. Samuel Sheppard, a Cleveland osteopath serving a life sentence as the convicted murderer of his wife, or grant him a new trial. (Dr. Sheppard was given a new trial and was acquitted). Among other reasons, the Supreme Court declared that three Cleveland newspapers had given Sheppard "inherently prejudicial publicity" in their news stories and in their editorial demands for Sheppard's conviction before he was brought to trial. In this case, the now trite yet important phrase, "trial by newspaper," was used frequently, thereby emphasizing on the public mind the conclusion that newspaper publicity can prejudice a jury.

The inherent danger to freedom of the press in this situation is that the newspaper has been ruled a threat to justice by our highest judicial body; and from this premise, one can then argue logically that the press must be controlled. In fact, the American Bar Association in October, 1966, adopted officially a resolution requesting the newspapers to invoke upon themselves a voluntary censorship regarding court cases. Under this resolution, the newspapers would present only the barest of facts about a case--being especially careful to withhold any fact that might prejudice a potential or an actual juror--until after a verdict is reached. If a given newspaper were to accept this resolution as a guideline, it would have chosen, in effect, to suppress news for a given period. Hence, it would have elected to curb freedom of expression.

How many newspapers will accept the practice as endorsed by the American Bar Association is, of course, anybody's guess. Nonetheless, one fact can be stated without qualification: the adoption of this practice will require the concerted action of all newspaper because few papers could afford to let competing newspapers print the story of arrests and trials while remaining silent themselves. The interest of the public in murders and similar stories is such that it can send newspaper circulation figures soaring. The situation is analogous to that of a restaurant that would refuse to serve coffee; it would be certain to lose many customers to other restaurants.

A less widely heralded legal threat to freedom of expression during the past decade turns on a single legal question: should the newspaper be compelled to reveal the sources of its information? Generally, the pattern has been one of a reporter obtaining an "inside" story (e.g., a leak from a city government employee regarding graft) which the newspaper carries. The newspaper, as a result of some subsequent legal action, is ordered by the sitting judge to state the source of its facts; the newspaper refuses, usually on the grounds of Constitutional rights and long standing precedent. The newspaper is then declared to be in contempt of court, and a round of trials, decisions, appeals, and further appeals follows. In 1964, for example, the _Philadelphia Evening Bulletin_ had to battle before the Pennsylvania

Superior Court to prevent the jailing of two of its staff members by a lower court for refusing to divulge the identity of the persons who provided the information for a municipal government scandal story; and in 1966, a co-ed editor of an Oregon college newspaper was held in contempt of court because she would not name the fellow students who gave her a confession story about their use of narcotics.

The right to conceal the source of a story from legal or other repercussion is, of course, an old and fiercely guarded concept. It is also a part of the foundation upon which the success of the modern newspaper rests. If it is taken away, the newspaper is certain to lose many of its best stories. More important to the newspaper, however, is the fact that any legal restriction in this area is also a legal control on freedom of expression.

In addition to the problems created by government and bar associations, the newspapers have faced the continuing necessity of avoiding offense to large racial, national, and religious groups. Any discussion of the racial strife of the past few years, for instance, must be so handled as not to offend any large group. This problem is becoming increasingly acute as these groups become more effectively organized and more able to put pressure on the newspaper through formal protest or, as they sometimes do, through boycott. Consequently these groups represent, in essence, an influence on--if not a direct threat to--freedom of expression.

Other attempts to place external controls on newspapers, and thus restrict freedom of expression, have come from individual citizens in many walks of life. Usually, the newspapers pay small heed to these attempts until they take the form of petitions to a legislature or other law-making body; then they generally rise up in concerted protest.

The demands of large or small parts of our citizenry to place controls on newspapers cannot be written off in every instance as narrowmindedness; on occasions, some newspapers have acted imprudently or foolishly. In the well known Red Scare of 1919-20, several newspapers are known to have falsified facts to heighten anti-Bolshevik feeling,[13] and even a cursory study of the history of many well known papers reveals that truth has sometimes been sacrificed to editorial policy. Some newspapers often abandon objectivity and fairness in the interest of larger circulation figures. When, for instance, the tabloid and the conventional newspaper with tabloid qualities cover the divorce proceedings of a movie actress or other well known personality, the treatment often unnecessarily emphasizes the unsavory or the seamy. Similarly, the picture editors of some newspapers place considerations of reader appeal above that of the subject's right to privacy, by using pictures of people sobbing at funerals, or displaying peculiar facial expressions in off-guard moments, or engaging in other activities which no reasonable person wants photographed.

The one check which society has invariably invoked upon the newspaper is the libel suit. Libel can be understood only loosely because its nature varies from State to State, and the term is in a constant state of redefinition. Broadly speaking. libel is a published attempt to defame by writing, printing, pictures, images, or any other means that appeals to the sense of vision; or stated in other terms, if one brings another into disrepute by means of published material, he is guilty of libel.

Because the only consistently successful defense against a libel suit has been to prove the statement true--

or in the case of pictures or other material (cartoons, etc.) to prove that no malice was intended and no injury done--newspapers have been held in check to some degree.

The matter of chain ownership is by no means a recent development. At the turn of the century, there were eight chains of major significance--Scripps-McRae, Hearst, Ochs, Booth, Kellow, Perkins, Pulitzer, and Belo--which controlled about ten percent of the daily circulation. Determining the exact number of chains at present is difficult because there is no common agreement on the number of papers which must be owned or controlled by a person or group before the designation of "chain" is applied. However, the number commonly given is in the upper forties. The single largest chain personage today is Samuel Newhouse[14] who owns or has the controlling interest in twenty-one newspapers.

The dangers of chain ownership are quite clear. One man or one group automatically obtains the attention of thousands of the reading public. If he desires, he can invent, color, distort, omit, or otherwise mislead on a large scale. When William Randolph Hearst claimed credit for launching the Spanish-American War, he was certainly making an excessive boast. Nonetheless, his claim is not to be dismissed lightly because his papers aided considerably in fanning the flames of war.

Within the past two decades, chain ownership has become even more dangerous since the chains now own and control other media of mass communication. Now, in addition to newspapers, the chain often owns several magazines and perhaps one or two radio and television stations. The seriousness of the situation is underlined by the fact that currently every "major" newspaper in the United States owns at least one radio station and, in most instances, a television station also.

V

A problem closely allied to those discussed above, which has grown within the past two decades, is the alarming increase in the number of one-newspaper cities--that is, cities which have only one newspaper for morning readers and one for evening readers. To make matters worse, both papers are frequently owned by the same person or group. The threat in this situation is, of course, that readers lose the benefit of contesting opinions from competing newspapers.

A typical example is Philadelphia, Pennsylvania, which is served by one morning paper, The Inquirer, one evening paper, The Evening Bulletin, and one tabloid, The Daily News, which strives to span the daylight hours. (To make matters worse, the same company owns both The Inquirer and The Daily News). In the early 1930's, The Inquirer was part of a three-way competition with two other papers, The Morning Ledger and The Record. The Morning Ledger "merged" with The Inquirer in 1934, and The Record fell victim to a union strike in 1946. Thus The Inquirer, formerly an openly Republican paper ranged against the Democratic Record, announced that henceforth it was to be "independent." It requires no specialist in semantics to realize that "independent" means simply a presentation of news as the editors see fit, unhampered by any considerations which the former competition might have presented.

The emergence of The Inquirer as the only morning

paper in Philadelphia paralleled the situation of The Evening Bulletin. At various times in its career, The Bulletin faced the competition of as many as four newspapers, most notably The Evening Ledger. These papers, however, folded one after the other, leaving the field to The Bulletin alone.

Because the situation in Philadelphia is typical of that of most American cities, the threat of a limited and sterile coverage everywhere is now a reality.[15]

Notes

1. Newspaper Rates & Data, Standard Rate & Data Service, Inc., Skokie, Illinois, November 12, 1969, p. 23.
2. Federal Responsibility for a Free and Competitive Press, International Typographical Union, Colorado Springs, Colorado, 1963, p. 112.
3. The first radio station in the United States appeared in East Pittsburgh, Pennsylvania, in 1921, and it was followed almost immediately by a mushroom growth of stations throughout the land. Actually, the first scheduled broadcast of news was given by this same station two months earlier when, in November, 1920, it gave the results in the Harding-Cox election.
4. Lippmann's influence was so great in 1967 that the President of the United States felt it necessary to try to refute Lippmann's view on the Viet Nam situation.
5. A businessman considering launching a newspaper to serve a town of 15,000 in southern New Jersey found, in April 1969, that he would have to spend approximately $500,000 in capital equipment alone.
6. In June, 1966, Ralph Ginsberg, publisher of several magazines including Eros, was denied by the U.S. Supreme Court any reconsideration of a fine and five years imprisonment for sending obscene material, specifically Eros, through the mails.

7. The Post Office can be made to capitulate by legal action. Grove Press, by carrying its case to the United States District Court, forced the Post Office to carry D.H. Lawrence's Lady Chatterly's Lover through the mails after the Post Office had steadfastly refused. (Grove Press v. Christenberry, 1959)

8. In October, 1966, the U.S. Supreme Court moved a little closer to a definition of "obscene" when it reversed decisions against specifically named booksellers for selling such works as Lust Pool and High Heels. In this same month, it upheld the right of the state of Arkansas to suppress and destroy such magazines as Gent, Bachelor, and Swank. In these decisions, the Court noted that there was an absence of "pandering" and "titillating" advertising, thereby anunciating at least one guideline for decisions.

9. President John F. Kennedy said of the press conference "It's like preparing for a final exam twice a month." Sorensen, Theodore C. Kennedy. N.Y., Harper & Row, 1965. p. 325.

10. To appreciate the difference between the situation described and the current situation, one need only note that in 1968 Harrison Salisbury, Pulitzer Prize winning writer of the New York Times, visited and interviewed the leaders of the North Viet Nam government when United States armed forces were at war with forces of that government. Then, on his return, he gave his views, by invitation, to the U.S. Senate.

11. A much more widely heralded but far less significant incident occurred when President Kennedy, in a fit of anger because of the treatment accorded him by the now defunct New York Herald-Tribune, cancelled the the White House subscription to that newspaper.

12. Parts of the trial of Jack Ruby for the murder of Lee Harvey Oswald, named by the Warren Commission as the assassin of President Kennedy, were broadcast live by radio. The reasoning was that the public had a right to first-hand knowledge of such a trial. A further interesting note is that Ruby shot and killed Oswald while television cameras were trained perfectly on the scene. Hence millions of persons witnessed the actual killing.

13. Murray, Robert K. *Red Scare*, Minneapolis, University of Minnesota Press, 1955.

14. A Briton, Lord Thomson of Fleet, actually owns more United States newspapers than Newhouse, but all of his American newspapers are in cities of populations of less than 125,000. Hence their influence is not nearly so great as that of the Newhouse chain. Thomson admits to owning or controlling "nearly 50" American newspapers.

15. For statistical proof, study the listings in the *Standard Rate & Data Service Yearbook, 1970.*

Chapter 2

The Newspaper in the Novel, 1900-30

I

The first intensive examination of American newspaper journalism in the twentieth century was occasioned by the rise of a group of magazine writers who were somewhat inaccurately called "muckrakers." This term, which is generally attributed to Theodore Roosevelt,[1] is taken from John Bunyan's Pilgrim's Progress where it refers to the character who, unmindful of the crown on his head, searches in the dirt for dross. The twentieth century muckrakers, one should note, were originally an idealistic group who used the printed word as a means to present the ills and the shortcomings of society for examination and possible correction. They should not be branded as a group interested primarily in exposing wrongdoing for personal gain or renown.

Muckraking derived its real impetus from McClure's Magazine which commissioned Ida M. Tarbell (1857-1944) at the turn of the century to write a series of articles on the Standard Oil Company of New Jersey. The major argument of these articles is that large corporations were outcompeting smaller groups and individuals through their ability to secure rebates from railroads. Miss Tarbell's work was only a starter for McClure's Magazine which immediately followed with articles by Lincoln Steffens (1866-1936) and Ray Stannard Baker (1870-1946). Steffens' most widely known work is The Shame of the Cities (1904), an exposé of the crime, graft, and illicit activities within city governments. Baker worked in the field opened by Miss Tarbell, later becoming an essayist under the pseudonym, David Grayson, and the official biographer of Woodrow Wilson.

The muckraking articles dealing with journalism turn, for the most part, on the thesis that the control of the newspaper was in the hands of the capitalists; that news was distorted, suppressed, or slanted to please the large businesses that advertised heavily in the newspapers; and that editorial policy was being diverted toward creating a favorable public image for big business. Although several muckraking articles on journalism appeared early in the century, the first really significant one was that of William Kittle, who, in an article on the Associated Press in the July 1909 issue of the _Arena,_ treats the subject of influences on editorial policy. A more widely read article, however, was Will Irwin's presentation in _Collier's,_ in 1911, of facts and figures to prove that the newspaper was sacrificing editorial integrity to business considerations. Two other widely read writings of the 1910-20 decade were the anonymous "Confessions of a Managing Editor" in the October 1914 issue of _Collier's_ and Maxwell Anderson's "The Blue Pencil" in the December 14, 1918 issue of the _New Republic._ The thesis of the _Collier's_ article is that the managing editor is controlled to a large degree by the business office which constantly scrutinizes advertising revenue; the thesis of Anderson's selection is that reporters and writers are not always free to express themselves openly--if they desire to hold their positions.

Because muckraking caught popular attention from its first appearance at the turn of the century, it naturally spread to the realm of fiction where it was employed with varying degrees of emotion, reason, and fervor. Among the novelists who relied on muckraking as a major element, the most prominent were Robert Herrick (1868-1938), David Graham Phillips (1867-1911), and Upton Sinclair (1878-1968).

Although Robert Herrick is associated with the muckrakers, he is actually a muckraker of a somewhat individual stripe. Fundamentally, he attempts to accomplish the difficult task of criticizing current conditions while creating novels and other writings possessed of the lasting qualities of great art. He also follows something of an individual pattern in his social criticism. Rather than single out institutions or practices for censure, he returns an indictment of the total system of which they are a part. Most often, he is concerned about the person of lofty values, of aesthetic sensitivities, and of creative inclinations who is swept aside by the all-powerful industrial, economic, and social structure. Thus Herrick in novel after novel condemns that structure in its entirety. (An exception is _Chimes_ (1925), a thinly veiled satire of the University of Chicago.)

To substantiate his broad condemnations, Herrick makes a searching analysis and careful evaluation of specific ills within the system he abhors. Yet he never makes any precise suggestions for reform. Instead, he confines his role to that of the deplorer.

Herrick's novels, in the main, reflect an unquestioned sincerity, an unusual analytical ability, and an unflagging industry. As he scores the American capitalistic system for binding men as individual personalities, he presents his case convincingly.

Probably because he rarely deals with specific institutions, Herrick never specifically condemns the American newspaper. His only mention of it, as in Memoirs of An American Citizen (1905) and Waste (1924), places it by implication within the Philistinism he disliked so intensely.

David Graham Phillips was an Indiana born newspaperman who worked for both the New York Sun and the New York World before becoming a freelance writer and later a novelist. A muckraker by instinct, Phillips was well equipped for his work. In addition to a well disciplined mind, he displayed a rare industry and solicitude for his writing; and he always sought out his material painstakingly and evaluated it judiciously in order to make as strong a case as possible. If his occasionally didactic tone detracts from the appeal of his work, his sincerity of conviction atones somewhat for the loss.

Phillips' first novel, The Great God Success (1901), is a carefully assembled if unevenly presented character study of Howard, a young journalist who sacrifices ideals for worldly renown. From an obscure beginning, Howard rises step by step to become a publisher, only to sell out to the coal trust at the height of his success. For his reward, he is made Ambassador to France.

The statement has often been made that Phillips invented Howard to satirize the career of Joseph Pulitzer, owner of the World, and as such, Phillips' one time employer. This conclusion cannot be given credence, however, for three reasons. First, Howard's life as a newspaperman bears a far closer resemblance to Phillips' career in journalism than to Pulitzer's. In fact, the novel has a strong autobiographical strain. Second, Pulitzer, in a cordial letter to Phillips, commended his former employee on the quality of the novel. And finally, the events in the novel that resemble Pulitzer's life and work also bear a likeness to the life and work of several other successful publishers.

The muckraking element in this novel is seen most strongly in Howard's lack of concern for others--especially his lowliest employees; in his unswerving pursuit of material wealth; and in his almost total disregard for the dignity of individual man. It is also clearly evident in a behavior pattern which Phillips assigns to Howard--that of a constant readiness to sacrifice human values for personal advancement. This pattern, one soon learns, is standard with Phillips; he fastens it with only slight variations on leading figures in all his muckraking works. And each time, he condemns it with a renewed vigor.

Phillips' only other treatment of the newspaper world in his almost thirty novels is a light one. He makes Emily Bromfield, the main character in <u>A Woman Ventures</u> (1902), a newspaper woman. The novel does not concern itself centrally, however, with journalism. It is, in actuality, a love story cast against a Park Avenue background, in which Emily is drawn to Marlowe, another reporter. Yet the story also creates a platform from which Phillips can pass judgment on the capitalistic system through the eyes of the newspaper personality.

As a reporter, Emily covers a variety of events, thereby enabling the author to speak through her--as he does, all too obviously. Emily, for example, covering a coal mining strike in Furnaceville, Pennsylvania, sounds like a tub-thumping radical as she and her colleagues blast mine owners, police, and everyone else who stands in the way of the miners.

Upton Sinclair became associated early in life with a socialist political philosophy and all that it embodies. For him, crusading for the rights of the proletariat came naturally; he appears to have found the perfect outlet for his talents.

At the opening of his career, he experienced a series of disappointments common to the beginning writer. Then suddenly he produced his most widely known novel, The Jungle (1906), which he intended as a strong condemnation of the manner in which the owners of the Chicago meat packing industries treated their employees. Actually, however, the book served more as an exposé of the methods used to slaughter animals and prepare meat for public consumption. The effect of the book was such that it became the greatest single force in effecting the passage of the Pure Food and Drug Act of 1906.

From an exposé and a denunciation of the meat packing industry, Sinclair made the easy step to a searching examination and strong indictment of many other facets of the capitalistic society he abhored. He belabored religious institutions, business, education, press, and every other suspected pillar of capitalism. His denunciations of journalism are to be found especially in his novel, Love's Pilgrimage (1911) and his extended tract, The Brass Check (1919).

In Love's Pilgrimage, a largely autobiographical work in which Sinclair scores education, religion and the arts, as well as journalism, the narrative element limps badly throughout. Sinclair trains his guns on the cold, business-like procedures which he finds in newspaper journalism; the well-being of the masses, he feels, is never a consideration in the publication of newspapers.

The Brass Check, which draws an analogy between prostitution and the press, is an indictment of the press for its failure, as Sinclair sees matters, to fill its rightful place in society. Sinclair sees the newspaper as forfeiting its rights on every hand to selfish interests of varying sorts. Specifically, he condemns the ownership of the nation's press by a few rich men who, aligned with other wealthy forces, tend to perpetuate the unfair system.

The principal devices used in The Brass Check are a first-person recounting of Sinclair's experiences with the press and a presentation of the findings of other persons whose views are the same. Hence this book is basically a combination of autobiography and reporting. In no sense is it literature in the context of "belles lettres."[2]

Over the years, Sinclair's views softened somewhat, but in every one of his many books that mention the press, he always sees it as the tool of the selfish interests that exploit the masses.

In addition to such outright muckrakers as Phillips, Herrick, and Sinclair, other novelists of the time employed muckraking elements in some of their writings. The most prominent of this group was Frank Norris (1870-1902) whose The Octopus (1901) and The Pit (1902) are clear attempts to expose the legal manipulations and flagrant dishonesty of dealers in wheat who conspired with railroads, business executives, and government figures to accomplish their purposes. Norris, of course, also wrote magazine articles in the muckraking vein. However, he never makes any extensive examination of newspaper journalism. He refers by implication to the power which the newspaper wields as an influence within society, and he uses newspaper people as characters. Yet, he never probes the subject in detail.

Norris comes closest to treating the institution of newspaper journalism in his novel Blix: A Love Idyll, published in 1899 but circulated principally in the twentieth century. In this work, the central figure, a newspaperman, falls in love with an attractive young woman of strong character. Thereafter, their lives become intertwined as they move against a background of California and New York.

The attempts to interpret journalism in this work, however, are few and superficial. Norris seems bent almost exclusively on explaining his characters in terms of his particular brand of naturalism. There are observations on newspaper work and newspaper ethics, but they are given only to explain the characters and their thoughts.

II

At the opening of the twentieth century, several of the established novelists had already done most of their best work. Hence they are sometimes viewed as novelists of the last century. Among this group, the most important are Mark Twain (1835-1910) and Henry James (1843-1916). In the second rank are William Dean Howells (1837-1920) and Hamlin Garland (1860-1940). In addition, there was a group who had begun their work before 1900 but were to reach their zenith in this century. Of this group, the most prominent are Edith Wharton (1862-1937), Theodore Dreiser (1871-1945), Ellen Glasgow (1874-1945), and Willa Cather (1876-1947). Because of the stature of these eight writers, their reactions to the newspaper are important to this study.

The work of Mark Twain has stirred controversy

among specialists in American literature since the early 1920's when interest in Twain suddenly assumed great proportions. All seem to agree that he is one of America's greatest novelists, but they disagree on the reasons. Most often, Twain is praised for the quality of The Adventures of Huckleberry Finn (1885), although many critics have attacked the structure of this acknowledged masterpiece.[3]

Specialists in American literature also agree largely on the sphere of interest in Twain's works. In his early writing, he displays a brand of rough Western humor and an earthy quality, as in "The Celebrated Jumping Frog of Calaveras County" (1865) and Roughing It (1872). From this humor, he drifted noticeably but not exclusively into satirical writing as in The Gilded Age (with Charles Dudley Warner, 1873) and several other works, the most widely known of which is A Connecticut Yankee in King Arthur's Court (1889). Thereafter, he seems to have become disillusioned, and his writings and other activities often exhibit a note of embitterment and declining interest in life itself.

In his satirical writings, Twain ridicules many customs and institutions. His Connecticut Yankee scores feudalism, class distinctions, privileges in the hands of the few, the church, and prominent philosophical concepts generally. In other writings, he blasts copyright laws, political organizations, capitalist figures and industrial giants, meantime championing the cause of the underdog and the downtrodden. Yet, like the other major novelists of his lifetime, he never attempted a thorough analysis of journalism, even though he, like so many others, had been a newspaperman and knew the world of the newspaper from inside.

Twain's broad understanding of the field of journalism

is reflected in a collection of six short stories entitled Editorial Wild Oats (1905). These stories--"My first Literary Venture," "Journalism in Tennessee," "Nicodemus Dodge--Printer," "Mr. Bloke's Item," "How I Edited an Agricultural Paper," and "The Killing of Julius Caesar"--are wonderfully entertaining. They exhibit the humor, the exaggeration, and the burlesque which Twain can employ so effectively; and at times they reveal, beneath the surface, the appealing satirical element of Connecticut Yankee and other works. Yet, despite Twain's knowledge of journalism and his unusual powers of discernment, he confines himself in these stories to recounting pleasant anecdotes and scenes rather than attempting to interpret any facet of the world of journalism.

Henry James stands in an almost unique position as a novelist with a strong sense of dedication. Always mindful of the power of the printed word, he was especially concerned about the influence of the novelist on society; and he was greatly troubled by the abrogation of that responsibility by many leading novelists. Instances of James' conception of the role of the novelist are reflected in his four well known prefaces (to Roderick Hudson, The American, Portrait of a Lady, and The Princess Casamassima) and in his widely reprinted essay, "The Art of Fiction." His views on this subject are also reflected in the famous public controversy which he carried on with H. G. Wells, novelist and historian of sorts.

James' concern with the influence of the novelist was heightened by his constant awareness of values. Although his principal interest is the novel of manners, especially as it treats the upper social levels, an accompanying interest should also be cited: James' novels reflect his concern for the individual of high moral values who must struggle within a society of lesser values. Quite often, James' central character attempts to move in a world where the values challenge his. James then proceeds to analyze his character against the milieu of that society. Isabel Archer in Portrait of a Lady, Christopher Newman in The American, and Daisy, the central character of Daisy Miller, are essentially well placed persons socially, moving in a social stratum where their values are tested constantly. In these characters and their movements, James evidences his interest in the necessity of high moral values, regardless of the difficulty one may experience in holding them.

James' direct criticisms of his native America are rather limited.[4] The reason is not, as is popularly assumed, that he chose to live abroad for most of his adult life, but that his themes transcend national cultures, thereby earning for him the designation of "international novelist." He was interested primarily in the deep inner meaning of life and the failure of many persons to understand that meaning. In The Bostonians he satirizes such American subjects as the women's suffrage movement, women's clubs, lecture devotees, and stuffy women such as Olive Chancellor who are so often associated with these facets of society. Also, in The American Scene, which is essentially a series of essays on places in the United States, he voices the dangers he perceives in the onrushing technology and its tendency to force aside all cultural considerations. Yet in the main, he was interested in institutions as they exist on an international rather than a national level. Consequently, when James chooses to focus attention on journalism--as in The

Reverberators (1888), a comedy of manners--he examines his subject in a manner that transcends national boundaries.

In this work, James casts the son of a cultivated South Carolina family residing in France as the admirer of a pretty American living close by. When they beoome engaged, newspapermen descend to obtain facts which the families consider private matters. This situation then gives James the opportunity to criticize the invasion of one's private life by modern journalism.

One can also see in this work James' attitude toward the newspaper and its role in society. He sees the newspaper as a deterrent against the forces which tend to raise man culturally because it fosters, rather than checks, public curiosity, inquisitiveness, and other questionable attributes of the masses.

James makes one other foray into the world of newspaper journalism in The Wings of the Dove (1902), a novel in which Merton Densher, one of his main characters, is a reporter for a London newspaper. However, although Densher serves as a working newspaperman in both the United States and his native Britain, he spends most of his time in non-journalistic activities in London and Vienna. James never deals at all extensively with Densher's newspaper work. His small observations on Densher the newspaperman include no philosophical treatment of journalism.

William Dean Howells, who at various times was quite friendly with both Twain and James, never treats the newspaper as an institution although he did publish a novel before the opening of the century recounting the life of a newspaperman. This work, A Modern Instance (1882), tells of Bartley Hubbard, a man who works on papers from Equity, a small New England town, to Whited Sepulchre, a community in Arizona.

In this novel, Howells displays a knowledge of journalism acquired from a lifelong association with newspapers and magazines. Yet except for occasional philosophizing about the work of a newspaperman, he makes no examination of the role of the newspaper as a force within our pattern of living. He merely recounts the experiences of a weak man of limited values who deserts his wife, tries vainly to divorce her, and finally, after a series of shoddy dealings, meets death at the hands of an irate citizen while serving as editor of a small newspaper. Consequently, this novel is merely another wherein the newspaper world is employed as the backdrop for a story.[5]

Hamlin Garland, short story writer and novelist, was much more deeply committed than Twain, James, or Howells to changing the political and economic system of his time, much more the castigator and the reformer. Born in Wisconsin but reared on farms in Iowa and South Dakota where his parents labored to eke out an existence, Garland was troubled by an established structure which, in his view, placed wealth and privilege in the hands of the few, while the many could hope only for bare subsistence and the highly improbable chance of their progeny having an easier lot. Life, in short, was a deck of stacked cards.

Garland became so exercised about the inequalities he saw that he turned from the writing of short stories, many of which are excellent, to the creation of novels that argue for his views. His _Jason Edwards: An Average Man_ (1892) is an open endorsement of the single tax theories of Henry George; _A Spoil of Office_ (1892) is a highly subjective portrayal of the history and value of the Populist Party; A Member of the Third Room (1892) is basically an exposé of power of the railroads in influencing legislation; and practically all his novels are drum-beaters in some respect for economic and social justice.

To accomplish his purposes, Garland employs a brand of realism which he himself termed "veritism." This term, as used by Garland, means a realistic approach and treatment designed to reveal the underlying truth of a given situation. Thus he was seeking to establish the real truth of the aspect of life under consideration at the moment. Although he often fails because he falls into the role of the propagandist or the mere denouncer, his novels have some moments of real quality, especially when his bitterness is relieved by an occasional note of optimistic romanticism.

Because Garland was interested in the problems which troubled the lower classes in his day, one might expect him to treat the institution of journalism either as an agent in suppressing the masses or as a means of arguing their cause. Yet he nowhere considers the place of the newspaper in society. This omission may be due to his preoccupation with more basic avenues by which the lower classes could achieve their ends. Hence he concentrates on political parties, legislation for social betterment, and the forces which imprison the masses directly, rather than examining such institutions as journalism which he felt played a secondary role.

Edith Wharton was well aware of the problems of the society about her, as is evidenced in The House of Mirth (1905), The Fruit of the Tree (1907), The Custom of the Country (1913), and The Age of Innocence (1920), all of which treat various phases of current social questions. Yet she always concentrates on the problem itself rather than examining the institutions behind it.

The House of Mirth involves the efforts of Rosedale, a Jewish financier, to rise in the social world, meanwhile presenting the difficulties encountered by Miss Lily Bart, whom Rosedale wants to marry, as she attempts to adjust her values to pressing economic necessities. *The Fruit of the Tree* depicts the struggle of a man to make his mill economically sound while he strives simultaneously to be a good father. In the same vein, *The Custom of the Country* examines the dichotomy that exists between the business man at his desk and in his home. Specifically, it raises again a question of values and condemns the American business man who concentrates on his workaday world to the exclusion of more important aspects of life.

Although Miss Wharton moves squarely into the business and industrial world of her time, she never treats the newspaper in any way. The difficulties and complexities faced by her characters do not touch the sphere of journalism.

Theodore Dreiser, like Garland, was aggravated to the point of bitterness about the social, economic, and political injustices which, as he saw matters, were victimizing the lower economic groups. However, he does not play the denouncer as bluntly in his novels as does Garland. He relies more on the approaches and the techniques of the standard novel, although he leaves no doubt in the reader's mind about his opinions.

Dreiser's six novels have made him one of the most controversial figures in the history of the American novel.

His most ardent supporters regard him as a genius; his detractors agree with the judgment of Lionel Trilling that he is over-rated.[6] No competent critic, however, disputes his significance in the development of the novel in America.

Dreiser, at his best, succeeds admirably in depicting a series of worlds wherein the central characters seem to be controlled by a social, economic, and biological determinism which makes them mere puppets; they are people who seem almost completely unable to swim against the strong currents into which they are cast by birth. This determinism has led many critics to brand Dreiser as a "naturalist," but the label is accurate only as a broad classification. Dreiser displays both a varying and a special brand of naturalism.

Dreiser was especially disturbed by the environmental forces which he saw at work in society. He was embittered by the economic injustice which denied the lower income group the opportunity to gain a decent living and practically precluded their rising in the world; he was very strong in his denunciation of the hypocrisy of the prevailing moral code; he abhored the tightening grip of big business and industry; and he was scathing in his appraisal of a political system which protected a small group at the expense of the masses. His novels, from _Sister Carrie_ (1900) to the post-humously published _The Bulwark_ (1946), are a series of stated and implied exposés, attacks, and diatribes against the forces which held men prisoners.

Although Dreiser attacks the moral code, the social system and the business world, he never singles out the newspaper for a prolonged analysis and consideration--although, as shown below, he does treat some phases of newspaper journalism rather thoroughly. Dreiser's failure to consider the institution of the newspaper more fully is surprising because of his close association with the newspaper and magazine world, and his demonstrated knowledge of everything therein. In his early years, he worked on newspapers in St. Louis, Chicago, and Pittsburgh; and thereafter he held a variety of positions on several magazines. These positions, which are treated extensively in his two autobiographical works (A Book About Myself, 1922, and Dawn, 1931), vividly portray the newspaper office and the newspaperman of Dreiser's era, but they do not treat the newspaper as an institution.

Dreiser's most extensive consideration of the newspaper and its role in society are to be found in the little asides in the two autobiographical works cited above and in his best known novel, An American Tragedy (1925). In A Book About Myself, for instance, he says of the St. Louis Globe-Democrat that "it was among the conventional of the conventional of its day (what American newspaper of that period could have been otherwise?) . . ." This statement is, of course, an implied criticism of the newspaper which allowed its editorial policy to be influenced from without.

In An American Tragedy, in which he displays the professional's knowledge of newspaper procedures and techniques, Dreiser condemns the practice of obtaining "news" at any cost and passing final judgments without concern for truth. As Clyde Griffiths sits in the courtroom, the newspapermen write and sketch with the almost total aim of feeding a gossip-hungry public; objectivity of presentation or fair treatment for the defendant never crosses their minds. Then, after the prosecutor delivers an emotional, distorted, and basically dishonest summation of his case, the newspapers carry highly biased headlines: "PROSECUTION IN GRIFFITHS' CASE CLOSES WITH IMPRESSIVE DELUGE OF TESTIMONY" and "MOTIVE AS WELL AS METHOD HAMMERED HOME." And when the unsound verdict is rendered, the newspapers "heralded everywhere" the fact that Clyde "had been properly convicted."

The final criticism of the newspaper in this widely read novel concerns dishonest procedures employed in news gathering. As Clyde sits in prison awaiting execution, his mother draws a "salary" from a newspaper as a "correspondent." She is decoyed into thinking that she is presenting bona fide news. Actually, she is simply displaying her innermost thoughts for the curiosity seekers and the savagely inclined busybodies who read the paper.

This novel stands, in essence, as an indictment of the newspaper as a co-partner with a prejudiced jury, organized religion, and society in general in condeming unjustly and exacting a cruel vengeance on one of its members.

Ellen Glasgow, who confines her writings almost exclusively to her native Virginia, is more of the social historian and less of the critic of specific conditions than Dreiser. She was especially concerned with the inability of the South to free itself from a blind adherence to the past and to adjust to the changes of the present; and in her depictions are an understanding and an insight that are truly unusual. Yet she always remains primarily the literary artist, interpreting the Virginia in which she was reared and which she held in lifelong affection.

Because the world of the newspaper had only a marginal influence on the Virginia world of Ellen Glasgow, there is very little treatment of institutions per se. Rather, there is a strong reliance on a narrative element that enables Miss Glasgow to interpret her characters as living people.

Willa Cather is a writer of unusual sensitivity who, like so many other American authors, sought for a spiritual unity in things American. Trained in journalism at the University of Nebraska, she worked on several newspapers and magazines, but she never chose to treat the institution of the American newspaper. The reasons seem clear enough. She found the source of her best novels in the mid- and far west in which she lived after her family moved from Virginia when she was only ten; she chose, for the most part, to delve into the past rather than to select from the contemporary scene; and she was interested in people rather than in institutions.

Also important in this regard is Miss Cather's conception of the role of the novelist. She felt that the true novel must be a work of art, and hence she strove to be an artist rather than a critic of activities. In her essay, "The Novel Demeuble,"[7] she says that the "novel is a form of imaginative art" and consequently "it cannot be at the same time a vivid and brilliant form of journalism." She also says, in her Not Under Forty (1936), "Every fine story must leave in the mind of the sensitive reader an intangible residuum of pleasure." These statements are indicative of her interest and the scope of her work.

By common consent, Miss Cather's best works are O Pioneers! (1913), the story of a peasant girl in the early days of Nebraska; The Song of the Lark (1915), a reconstruction of the frontier community which Miss Cather knew as a small girl; My Ántonia (1918), the story of the struggle of an immigrant girl; and Death Comes for the Archbishop (1927), the story of a priest in the Southwest in the immediate post-Mexican War days. In each of these novels, the scene is the mid- or far west, and except for My Ántonia, the time is remote from the present.

Miss Cather was acutely aware of environment as a strong influence on mankind, and she was deeply knowledgeable in the qualities which comprise human nature. With her knowledge of journalism, had she chosen to do so, she might well have examined the institution of the newspaper quite capably.

III

During these first two decades of the twentieth century, many minor novelists treated some aspect of newspaper journalism. Usually, they chose a newspaperman for a central or an important character and then depicted him in terms of his work. At other times, however, they also attempted to interpret one or more phases of the newspaper world. The following discussion covers the most important and the most representative of these lesser novels of the period.[8]

In 1901, Albert Bigelow Paine published his The Bread Line: A Story of a Paper, an entertaining account of four enterprising young men who started a newspaper in New York, only to find themselves bankrupt a year later.

The story is basically humorous, but it portrays rather effectively the inherent dangers of the time in launching a newspaper. The four entrepreneurs have not reckoned with the ingrained habits of the reading public, the difficulties of pleasing readers on all levels, and the many other enigmatic conditions which have always presented thorny problems for anyone starting a newspaper--or even for those running long established newspapers. Thus the four fall victim to their own naiveté.

Aside from the understanding demonstrated in the business considerations of the newspaper, however, this novel has little to offer in the way of interpretation of newspaper journalism.

In 1905, Joseph A. Altsheler presented his *Guthrie of the Times,* a character study of a journalist of high ideals. Although the author names no particular location, the setting is easily recognized as the state of Kentucky.

The principal action deals with the central character's long but successful attempt to prevent the impeaching of a public official by a ruthless financial enterprise. In the process of achieving victory, Guthrie earns the admiration of his fellow citizens--and, especially important to the author, also gains a beautiful wife.

Although the author displays a thorough knowledge of journalism, he weakens his story by his oppressive moral tone. Over and over, he states or implies that the newspaperman need not be a yellow journalist--that one can move on an ethical plane even if he is a newspaperman. Thus he permits his didactic tone to prevail at the expense of a warmly and sympathetically drawn character.

The importance of this novel is purely historical. It was widely read and accepted as a representative portrayal of activities and thoughts in the newspaper world.

The following year, 1906, four novels worth noting appeared. They are Jesse L. Williams' *The Day Dreamer,* Olin L. Lyman's *Micky,* and Miriam Michelson's two works,

Anthony Overman and Yellow Journalist.

The importance of The Day Dreamer lies in the author's success in capturing the atmosphere of the city room. As a newspaperman Williams was in a position to know that atmosphere as the professional actor comes to know the stage and the sculptor the studio, and he depicts it effectively in a clear and readable style.

The importance of Lyman's Micky arises from its author's clear understanding of journalistic talent. This novel recounts the story of Michael O'Bryn, a drifter who begs for and obtains a position as a reporter on the Daily Courier. By virtue of great native talent, he becomes a hit almost immediately and handles only the most important of stories. An old tendency toward drunkenness, however, re-asserts itself, and this weakness, together with a shattered romance, sends him adrift once more in quest of the grip on life which he has never obtained.

Although this story is simply told, it reflects an unmistakable warmth. Micky is sympathetically and understandingly drawn against a background of newspaper practices and conversations. The story is also significant for the manner in which the author handles the old question: are newspapermen born or made? He says, convincingly, through his characterization of Micky, that one either has the necessary talent or has not, and that one rises in direct proportion to his talent.

The importance of Miss Michelson's two works is that they emphasized the bad light in which many citizens already saw the institution of newspaper journalism.

In Anthony Overman, Miss Michelson depicts the newspaper as an essentially profit-hungry institution, ever ready to sacrifice any lofty purpose for financial gain. Overman is both actor and philosopher, and through him and his speech, the author gives the newspaperman, the newspaper, and every other phase of journalism a very low rating.

Yellow Journalist is an even stronger indictment of the newspaper world. The central character is a young woman reporter who invariably places obtaining a story above any ethical consideration. She never hesitates to listen at keyholes, to deceive, to lie, or to cheat in her quest of news. The story concludes by having her relinquish her career to marry a rival reporter, thereby creating something of a human touch. Yet the reader can never free himself of the picture of a scheming and furtive little vixen who belongs in a class with the card sharp or the swindler.

There can be little doubt that Miss Michelson drew her characters from real life prototypes. Nor can one doubt her knowledge of yellow journalism. Her novels stand, despite revolting overtones, as a competent portrayal of a particular kind of journalism. The unfortunate aspect is that the uninformed reader might tend to accept these portrayals as representative of a large part or all of the newspaper world.

Between 1909 and 1915, four novels bearing on newspaper practices were published: William R. Hereford's The Demagog (1909), Henry S. Harrison's Queed (1911), Samuel H. Adams Clarion (1914), and David Grayson's Hempfield (1915).

The most striking aspect of The Demagog is its strong parallel to the life of William Randolph Hearst. The central character, like Hearst, is the owner of a chain of newspapers. Like Hearst also, he has strong convictions accompanied by unrelenting determination and ethically questionable behavior. Finally, like Hearst, he has Presidential ambitions.

In his efforts to gain the office, he is without principle. He feels no compunction about engaging in flagrant deceptions and ward level trickery. But more important, he uses his newspapers as a powerful weapon in his endeavors. In the end, however, his knavery is his undoing, and he falls impotently into the background.

Stating Hereford's purpose in creating this novel is difficult. Nonetheless, the fact is clear that it aroused its readers to a danger of chain ownership: the potential for wide promotion of an intrinsically evil cause.

Harrison's Queed is another indictment of yellow journalism. The main character, a man of twenty-four, works in the editorial department of a Southern paper which is squarely in the yellow journalism camp. Disillusioned completely by his attempts to raise the standards of his paper, he falters badly in his attempt to face life itself. Only by the efforts of the young lady whom he loves is he able to save himself as he retires from the newspaper scene, an emotionally battered young man.

The importance of this novel is simply that as a rather carefully written case against yellow journalism, it had a heavy impact on the reading public of its time. Thus it assisted in creating popular ideas regarding journalism which have remained through the years.

Adams' Clarion turns on a very delicate conflict within the realm of editorial policy--the conflict between responsibility to one's family and to sound journalistic practices.

In this story, Hal Surtaine, the only son of a man made rich by selling a quack medicine, buys and becomes the publisher of the Clarion, a newspaper in his family's home town. Before long, however, he faces a soul-searching test when his paper, pursuing its editorial policy of safeguarding the public interest, decides to run an exposé of his father's dishonesty. Hal eventually rules in favor of established editorial policy, but not without great emotional strain.

Although this novel exhibits a firm knowledge of editorial practices and journalism generally, it still concerns itself principally with the characters as human beings. Its significance in terms of journalism lies in its treatment of a type of conflict which any newspaper publisher might have to face. Obviously, every publisher does not meet these precise circumstances, but he may well encounter a conflict between his editorial policy and the activities of a clergyman within his church, an official within his Alma Mater, or perhaps even a dishonest person within a local charitable organization.

Grayson's Hempfield is essentially an argument for editorial policy based on the upright life. In this novel, a young lady named Anthy inherits her father's weekly newspaper and, assisted by a group of interesting characters, assumes the role of publisher. Of the group, the most influential is Nort Carr, an intellectual printer who longs to revolutionize the paper and the entire institution of journalism by concentrating on truth.

One cannot escape the author's unbounded optimism. He feels that goodness is the only antidote for the evils of the world. If only newspaper editors and others in a position to sway the masses would concentrate on the moral life, he seems to say, all would soon be well.

The weakness of Grayson's argument is that he oversimplifies the complex issues of editorial policy. A newspaper following his recommendation would soon lose reader appeal, circulation, and advertising revenue.

Because of Grayson's following, his novel was read widely, but it had little lasting effect. It was read and mostly forgotten.

IV

In addition to these treatments of journalism, there were other novels within this time span which employ newspapermen as characters without delving much beneath the surface of the newspaper world.

The newspaperman appears as a character in a number of novels of the period which have a serious purpose. For example, Roy R. Gilson's Miss Primrose (1906) employs Butters, an editor, as a personality to accentuate the lovable and altruistic qualities in the central figure, Letitia Primrose. George C. Eggleston uses a newspaperman as one of a group striving valiantly in Blind Alleys (1906) to help the downtrodden of New York. Charles A. MacLean's The Mainspring (1912) casts a newspaperman as the main character fighting a gigantic financial interest for possession of a New York railroad. Cynthia Stockley tells the story in Wanderfoot (1914) of the love story of a famous surgeon and a newspaper woman who marry, separate, and re-unite (all with little mention of the newspaper world). Jerome K. Jerome's All Roads Lead to Calvary (1919) has Joan Allway, a journalism major, dedicate herself to a life of religious service because of a sermon she hears based on the text used as the title for the novel.

Newspapermen are also to be found in some of the period's humorous novels. George Horace Lorimer's False Gods (1906) employs a reporter, appropriately named Simpkins, as a central character in a narrative wherein a beautiful woman misleads him as he seeks a story. He follows a trail that involves Egyptian mysteries, statues that seem human, black cats, and supposed crime, finally falling victim to a carefully devised plan to befuddle him. Wilbur D. Nesbit's Gentleman Ragman (1906) tells the story of a newspaper office boy, Johnny Thompson, who recounts private information about his editor, his editor's friends, and the citizens of Plainville--all in the strikingly humorous manner of an appealing and forthright adolescent. Alexander Otis' Hearts Are Trumps (1909) recounts the humorous experiences of Basil Plympton, a New York newspaperman, who exchanges identities with a clergyman. William J. Locke's Jaffrey (1915) has Jaffrey Chayne, a war correspondent, return from the Balkans with a widow bequeathed to him by a dying companion.

Newspapermen also appear as characters in children's and adolescent's literature. Two examples can suffice from a long list where newspapermen make a prolonged or short-lived appearance. In Alice Caldwell Rice's Mr. Opp (1909), the title character is the owner and publisher of the Opp Eagle. In Walter P. Eaton's Peanut--Cub Reporter, one of a series of "Peanut" stories, the central character grows to early manhood and begins a career in newspaper work on a New York daily.

A final use of newspapermen as characters in this period is that of the newspaperman as narrator. Quite often, a newspaperman had a true or semi-true story to tell, and he chose a journalist as narrator. An example is Will L. Comfort's Red Fleece (1915) in which the newspaperman narrator, Peter Mowbray, follows the war from behind the Russian lines and philosophizes upon the absurdity of war.

V

The 1920's were a time, critics seem to agree, of both rebellion and iconoclasm. In the early part of the decade, the disillusionment that followed World War I was widespread, accompanied by a clear disdain for idealism in general. Frederick J. Hoffman says of the time[9]

> The mood of futility, the shrugging of shoulders over questions of moral imperative, were in large part a consequence of the war. The postwar generation felt honestly that it had been victimized by a gross and stupid deception. Nothing genuine had come out of the war . . . .
>
> The public personality, because he was public and spoke in platitudes became ridiculous; and along with him, the sponsors of 'ideals' and 'values' . . . were thrown into discard

Leon Howard says of the literary expression of this period[10]

> No period in American history, perhaps, gave greater encouragement to freedom in literary expression, but it was the freedom of iconoclasm rather than that of inspiration.

As the decade progressed and the cities assumed new power and greater size, a certain antipathy to the small town, the narrowness of the preceding age, and a general revolt against older concepts also evolved. This revolt, aided by the headiness and the prosperity of the times, remained strong until shaken by the sudden appearance of the depression, the origin of which is commonly associated with the stock market crash of 1929.

In such an atmosphere, there was a natural tendency to ferret out reality behind the facade of social respectability, to expose sham and pretense in high place, and to cast a strong light into every corner of hallowed structures. This tendency, therefore, reflected itself strongly in much of the literature of the period.

Of the writers commonly associated with the 1920's, the most important are Sherwood Anderson (1876-1941), Sinclair Lewis (1885-1951), and F. Scott Fitzgerald (1896-1940). In addition, of course, other major writers already discussed (e.g., Theodore Dreiser and Edith Wharton) and others to be discussed (e.g., Ernest Hemingway and William Faulkner) were writing during this decade. They, however, are not thought of as part of the 1920's in the sense that Anderson, Lewis, and Fitzgerald are associated with this decade.

Sherwood Anderson is fundamentally interested in examining individual character against the machine age. Concentrating principally on the middle and lower social classes of his native midwest America, he is preoccupied with the imprisonment of personality by the forces which are at work in society. Specifically, he condemns most often the creeping technology and the enslaving effects of a bland conventionality. He sees both the rural and the urban community as a vast series of traps into which man is certain to fall, with little or no hope of extricating himself. Again and again, as in his _Winesburg, Ohio_ stories, he singles out the forces which he feels are part of the traps. He cites the crippling social strictures which force young people into the wrong marriages; he rails against the economic fetters which bind a George Willard; and he scores the morass of man-made cultural bogs to be met everywhere.

Classifying Anderson according to his treatment of the newspaper is quite simple; he is another author who makes no examination of the institution of journalism but does use a character from the newspaper world occasionally. Among such characters the most prominent is Bruce Dudley, who changed his name from John Stockton, the central personality in Anderson's novel _Dark Laughter_ (1925).

Dudley is a man of shallow values and small drive. Leaving his position as a reporter for a Chicago newspaper and deserting his wife Bernice, he falls into a job as wheel varnisher in a factory, followed by a short period as a gardner and a routine worker in other small jobs. Meanwhile, he has an affair with his employer's wife, sinks into a listless existence, and loses the battle with life generally.

In _Dark Laughter_ there is no real interpretation of the newspaper or the role of the newspaperman. Rather, like so many other novelists, Anderson seems simply to have chosen the newspaper world as an appropriate background for part of a particular story.

Sinclair Lewis is the author of twenty books and several unpublished sketches and other material found among his papers after his death. Of the twenty books, most are novels, while the others are collections of short stories, plays, and essays. Yet, despite Lewis' almost total use of contemporary American material, he never attempts a full length depiction of a newspaperman or any extensive consideration of the newspaper.

Lewis's failure to deal with matters of journalism is especially significant because of his deep commitment to a criticism of his age. He objected to the materialism of the time, to the intellectual dearth, and to everything that, in his judgment, tended to stifle lofty values. He expressed his feelings pointedly and, at times, almost vehemently. His Main Street (1920), for example, burns small town America to the ground. Herein he scorns the desire for social position, the pettiness, and above all, the cultural void which he saw everywhere--but especially in the small town. Carol Kennicott, the central character, is simply one little voice drowned out by the raucous mass as she tries vainly to raise the cultural tone of her husband's mid-west community. In Babbitt (1922), Lewis satirizes the narrowness of the American business man whose values, he believes, constitute a threat to a sound society. Those values, Lewis holds, are wrong because they emphasize materialism and self-interest but find no place for aesthetic considerations or for the humanizing effects of culture. In Kingsblood Royal (1947), he explores a pernicious vein in the area of race relations. And in most of his other works, Lewis continues to attack materialism, shortsightedness, and other conditions of his time and place, striving constantly to make his age hold the mirror up to itself. Because of this interest, one would certainly expect Lewis to treat the newspaper as a contributing force to the conditions he satirizes--but this treatment never materializes.

Lewis' failure to deal with matters of journalism is also striking because he knew the newspaper from the inside. As a beginning writer, he worked on Connecticut newspapers as a full time reporter, and later as a magazine and book publishing house editor, he had further contacts with newspapers and newspapermen. In addition, this personal experience was reinforced by marriage to one of America's leading newspaper personalities, Dorothy Thompson, who was his wife from 1928 to 1942. Certainly, therefore, he had an extensive opportunity to discern the influence of the newspaper on our way of life--all of which could have led logically to some kind of evaluation.

F. Scott Fitzgerald was of all the novelists of the 1920's the most directly committed to his time. In fact, he deals with his time to such an extent that he is often termed somewhat inaccurately the "laureate of the Jazz Age."

Overpraised in the Twenties and generally underestimated in the next three decades, Fitzgerald has now been re-assessed with a surprising degree of unanimity of judgment. The superb artistry of _The Great Gatsby_ (1925) is now widely acclaimed, as are the best passages of _The Last Tycoon,_ the novel upon which Fitzgerald was at work when death came. Meanwhile, the technical weaknesses and the other shortcomings of _This Side of Paradise_ and other writings are conceded by the most ardent of Fitzgerald devotees. Fitzgerald, at his best, interprets his characters with a sensitivity and a beauty that are genuinely compelling; but in his lesser writings he leaves loose ends hanging and important questions and areas unexamined.

Fitzgerald restricted his subject matter to a narrow life within his own time. He focused on the upper social levels of eastern United States, particularly the New York area, concerning himself especially with people within that group who strove unsuccessfully to adjust to their world. Persons from other levels make an appearance in Fitzgerald novels--as for example, George and Myrtle Wilson, the automobile mechanic and his wife in The Great Gatsby--but they appear only to round out the story of a character from an upper level.

Fitzgerald, in short, was preoccupied with a given social stratum and its immediate concerns, and therefore, he was interested only in the institutions that touched directly the lives within that stratum. Because journalism had no special place in their lives, it is not treated in his works.

VI

During the 1920's, several second and third level novelists attempted to treat one or more phases of newspaper journalism but generally achieved little more than moderate success. As one examines these novels, he sees their weaknesses rather clearly. Frequently, they have structural or factual shortcomings; but more often, they lack the insight and the artistry characteristic of the unusual production. Yet many of them had, in their time, a surprisingly large reading public. The following is a discussion of the most important of these works.

Samuel H. Adams produced two novels within two years that center their stories in the newspaper world. The first, published before the decade opened, is Common Cause (1919); the second is Success (1921). Common Cause concerns itself with the story of Jeremy Robson, a young reporter working in a heavily pro-German area during World War I. His newspaper, motivated by selfish editorial policy interests, caters to local sentiment by foregoing accuracy of interpretation and loyalty to one's own government in order to sell papers. Robson, who is cast in the Horatio Alger mold, rebels but achieves no real success; he never seriously alters his paper's policies or practices.

This book, a thinly disguised interpretation of the Wisconsin area of the time, has little special merit. It is simply another attack on the practice of some newspapers of compromising editorial policy in the interest of circulation figures--as well as something of a flag waving call for patriotism.

Adams' second book, Success, had a wider and more receptive audience than his first, and therefore had greater influence on the reading public. Revolving about the activities and thoughts of Errol Banneker, a young westerner working in New York as a reporter, it is a strong and blatant attack on yellow journalism. Banneker--idealistic, industrious, uncompromising--works his way from lowly reporter to editor-in-chief, only to find himself controlled by the demands of yellow journalism and outside pressures on editorial policy. His high minded editorials are nullified by the cheap and often licentious material on the surrounding pages; and his pleas for lofty journalism are only a small voice in the wind. Then, when certain "important" advertisers object to his editorials, he is given a cease and desist order from the top office. Banneker, defeated and disillusioned, returns with his newly acquired wife to the desert area from whence he came to mull over his defeat.

The situation depicted in this novel is rather seriously overdrawn. Adams indicts, but with hit-and-run tactics. He seems intent on arguing that the newspaper created by him is representative of all papers, that the journalism of Success is the journalism found throughout the nation. As a result, one has the feeling upon closing this novel that he has read another work squarely in the muckraking, rather than the artistic, tradition.

Sidney C. Williams' The Unconscious Crusader (1920) has one element in common with Adams' Success: each is an attempt to create a high minded, altruistic journalist around whom to recount a story and to praise a lofty brand of journalism. In the fate of their central characters, however, there is a sharp difference.

In The Unconscious Crusader, James Radbourne, a hard, clean fighter resolves from the moment that he becomes a beginning reporter to strive to uplift the entire institution of journalism. His method is simply to make himself and his journalistic work examples of lofty values. When, after years of unceasing work, he becomes an editor, he remains true to his commitment, producing a paper characterized by his philosophy.

Although this novel represents only adequate achievement, it does picture realistically and authentically many of the subtleties of the question of reader appeal versus loftiness of tone. No editor or editorial policy committee can establish final guidelines on this question. Yet neither can they ever cease to try.

Clarence B. Kelland's Contraband (1923) is a fairly convincing portrayal of the power which a newspaper can exert in fighting for a cause. The novel recounts the story of Carmel Lee, a capable and determined young lady who inherits a small town newspaper and then uses it to fight municipal corruption and crime. In the aftermath, she slugs toe to toe with Abner Fownes, the war lord of the corruption.

The book is exciting in spots and interestingly written but otherwise lacking in any unusual quality. Nonetheless, it reflects what a newspaper can do to check wrongdoing in any quarter.

Two novels of the year 1924, You Too by Roger Burlingame and The Hoarding by John Owen, treat the subject of advertising. In You Too, the central character, Gail Winbourne, a man of literary aspirations and high morality, is forced into the advertising business where he becomes deeply upset by the deception and lack of moral concern which he finds in newspaper and other advertising. In The Hoarding, advertising ethics is also treated, although not in so extensive or so philosophical a manner as in You Too.

In examining the subject of advertising ethics as handled in these two works, one must remember that it was much more of a problem in the 1920's than at present. The reason is that since that time most national associations of advertising agencies and newspaper publishers have adopted codes insuring higher ethical standards. Therefore, fraudulent and deceptive advertising has decreased sharply over the last few decades.

Edwin H. Lewis' Sallie's Newspaper (1924) focuses attention on the subtleties of editorial policy. Sallie Flower, a young millionairess, decides to make two changes in the editorial procedures of the Seganku (Wisconsin) Daily Sun, which she owns. She makes a sharp change in the paper's format, and she suddenly points the editorial policy toward improving the public image of Dromillard Schmidt, the man the town expects her to marry. Her editor, Jim Fletcher, aids in her plan--against his better judgment and despite his love for Sallie. When the whole venture proves disastrous, Sallie has to admit defeat, and Jim resigns to become a mere farmhand.

Although this novel has no claim to greatness, its

author demonstrates a clear perception of the inherent dangers of changing editorial policy without thorough consideration. Editorial policy, as both Sallie and Jim learn, is a highly complex matter, fraught with all manner of booby traps and other hidden perils. The paper which treats it lightly is the paper which is courting trouble.

Henry Justin Smith's Josslyn (1924), a study of a newspaper personality, is the kind of novel that is likely to be midjudged. It is not especially well written, nor does it reflect any great powers of portraiture. Yet it is unusually successful in treating a fact well known to the true journalist: a sufficiently strong personality can meet the challenges of modern journalism and derive both satisfaction and pleasure from the encounter.

Josslyn, the sensitive but inwardly strong son of a college professor, finds himself as a working newspaperman in the worst atmospheres of metropolitan Chicago. He meets people from the lowest walks of life, under the most trying of conditions; he must face constantly a variety of dangers, pressures, and personal strain. Yet, by virtue of a sound philosophy, a healthy personality, and a firm conviction of the importance of the newspaper in society, he comes through successfully.

If this novel does nothing else, it serves to refute the all too common belief that most newspapermen are failures, cynics, or misfits, and if they are not in such a category when they enter the newspaper world, the nature of the work therein will soon cast them beyond the pale of "normal" society.

Edward Hungerford's Copy Shop (1925) possesses a degree of historical interest. The novel turns on the story of Wendell P. Groome, a callow young man from Uxdale, New York, who has two dominant attributes: an unshakable stubbornness and a skill in promoting himself as a man of talent and ability. After serving on The Tremont Republic, he moves to The New York Planet (an obvious parody on The New York Sun), from whence he rises to become editor of The Republic, a large and influential publication.

The appeal of this novel lies principally in its graphic portrayal of The Sun of the first decade of the twentieth century. The central personalities, the editorial policy, and the peculiar atmosphere of that important paper are drawn skillfully and convincingly. In addition, the atmosphere of the city room of The Sun is reproduced so competently that one can sense much of the news gathering and editing procedures of the time.

Clara Sharpe Hough's Not for Publication (1927) is a fairly competent treatment of the pressure of blackmail which, in some instances, has been applied to newspapers. Serena Morley, who owns most of the stock in The Banner, a New England daily, is happily married to Dave, editor of the paper. Their happiness, however, is interrupted by the appearance of Tony, an old suitor of Serena's, who is now a big time bootlegger. Difficulties arise because The Banner, learning of Tony's activities, is suddenly faced with an unexpected pressure: Tony threatens to make public a compromising letter received from Serena in days past if the paper says anything unfavorable about him. Serena pleads with Dave to accede to the demand, but Dave, true to his newspaperman's sense of truth, refuses.

Although the facts of this story are somewhat melodramatic and although such pressures are more rare these days, the situation is still basically sound. Many newspapers of the present, especially small papers, are forced to bow to demands that are less obvious and less dramatic. Hence they are, in effect, the victims of a milder form of blackmail. Some examples are the small newspaper which dares not print any fact disparaging a large national group in its location, even though the fact be true; the newspaper that must run a story of a dull event simply to please a person or group; and the newspaper that dares not support any legislation (e.g., a tax on jewelry) that runs counter to a narrow, selfish local interest.

Malcolm H. Ross' Penny Dreadful (1929) has a limited significance as a treatment of the tabloid's lack of ethics and related problems. Ruth North, a sob sister on a tabloid, writes a series of vindictive accounts of her ex-husband and his present love. The tabloid, in the interest of circulation figures, overlooks the spleen and flagrant lack of taste in the writings. However, the articles backfire as Ruth becomes the laughing stock of the community and the tabloid loses face for carrying the articles.

VII

During this decade, there were also, as is to be expected, several novels which used newspapermen as characters. Two examples can illustrate the situation.

Wayland W. Williams' Goshen Street (1920) is a story wherein one of the principals in a boy-meets-girl situation is a newspaperman. David Galt, a fine, upright young man, is sent to college through the generosity of a millionaire in his Connecticut neighborhood. After graduation, Galt, now deeply hopeful of winning Sylvia Thornton, the daughter of his benefactor, becomes a newspaperman and then a soldier in World War I. The course of his love for Sylvia, however, is interrupted by his marriage to Naomi Fiske who dies during the influenza epidemic. Shortly thereafter, he returns to his Goshen Street home and Sylvia.

Louis Dodge's Whispers (1920) is another of the many mystery stories which employ a newspaperman as a central character. In this work, reporter Robert Estabrook, who has been named "Whispers" by a hardened city editor because of a speech defect, announces upon being hired that he will solve within two days the mystery surrounding the death of old Pheneas Drum. Naturally, he is as good as his word.

Notes

1. President Roosevelt used the phrase in his speech at the laying of the cornerstone of the House of Representatives in 1906.

2. The pattern of the attack on the press made by Sinclair in The Brass Check was made most notably in the early part of the century by Will Irwin in an article in Collier's magazine in 1911. More recently, it was made by George Seldes in Freedom of the Press (1935) and Lords of the Press (1938). Seldes, a foreign correspondent of considerable stature, sees the press under the control of a small group with selfish interests.

3. An example is William Van O'Connor's "Why Huckleberry Finn is Not the Great American Novel," College English XVII (October 1955).

4. Henry James' friend and fellow novelist, Edith Wharton, chided him lightly (see her A Backward Glance, p. 176). for his failure to "depict the American money-maker in action."

5. Howells best displays his knowledge of journalism as an institution in Criticism and Fiction (p. 290-309) and Literature and Life (p. 63-77).

6. Trilling, Lionel. The Liberal Imagination, New York, Viking Press, 1950. p. 9.

7. The New Republic Supplement, April 1922.

8. Two works published in 1899 but circulated principally in this century should be noted. The first is Booth Tarkington's The Gentlemen from Indiana; the second is Jesse L. Williams' The Stolen Story, And Other Newspaper Stories. The latter is a collection of related anecdotes and philosophical observations of the New York newspaper world. It is authentic, readable, and appealing, and undoubtedly heavily autobiographical.

9. The Twenties, Collier Books, New York, 1962, p. 99 and p. 75.

10. Literature and the American Tradition, Doubleday & Co., New York, 1960, p. 264.

Chapter 3

The Newspaper in the Novel, 1930-50

I

Any consideration of the United States of the 1930's inevitably turns on the great depression and all that it entailed--the closing banks, the fading businesses, the destitute, the hungry, and perhaps above all, the thousands upon thousands of citizens who passed through successive stages of shock, bewilderment and resentment to demands for corrective action. The corrective action demanded came largely, of course, in the form of legislation commonly associated in the popular mind with the New Deal and Franklin D. Roosevelt.

In making demands for action, most of the citizenry looked naturally to the newspapers for assistance. They wanted the papers to print their grievances and to call editorially for legislation to relieve the general situation. When the newspaper was suspected of failing to carry the banner of the oppressed, it was condemned vigorously by the general populace.

Meanwhile, in some quarters there was resentment of another kind against the newspaper. It was a resentment arising from the settled conviction that the newspapers were at least partially responsible for allowing the wealth to fall into the hands of the few. The reasoning behind this conviction was that the newspapers withheld criticism of big business in order to obtain revenue from advertisements, thereby enabling big business to take unfair advantage of the general public. Hence the newspaper was actually a partner in the crime of making the rich richer and the poor poorer. This idea, which was given such emphasis by the muckrakers at the beginning of the century, has persisted to this day, despite the fact that it requires extensive qualification.

Because of the conditions of the 1930's, the appearance of the novel that criticizes institutions, pleads causes, or otherwise renders a judgment on the injustices and the shortcomings of an age seems only natural. The novel reflecting these aims in that particular decade was variously termed the "novel of social criticism," the "novel of social history," and the "Proletarian Novel." This novel existed, of course, beside those written in the traditional pattern of the pure narrative, as well as those conceived in other structural patterns and with other basic aims.

The novelists who figured most prominently in the 1930's are John Dos Passos (1896-), William Faulkner (1897-1962), Ernest Hemingway (1899-1961), Thomas Wolfe (1900-1938), and James T. Farrell (1904-). Although each of these writers has several full length works to his credit, they venture only peripherally into the world of journalism.

In John Dos Passos, one finds an interesting use of items and people from the world of journalism but only scattered attempts at interpretation of the newspaper itself. This fact is surprising because of Dos Passos' association with journalism and his all-pervading concern with the social and economic conditions which he regarded as pernicious to the masses.[1]

In his well known trilogy, U. S. A.--which is comprised of his The 42nd Parallel (1930), 1919 (1932), and The Big Money (1936)--Dos Passos turns to the newspaper, the newsreel, the magazine, the radio newscast, and other devices of mass communication to portray the social, political, and economic history of the United States from the beginning of the century to the depression of the 1930's. In this trilogy, he clearly implies a criticism of our entire order and because of the devices and techniques employed in this work, some critics argue that Dos Passos is at least as much a writer of tracts as a novelist. He sees an alarming portent in a system that gives a small group more wealth than it needs while denying to the masses the necessities of life. In essence, he calls for a social revolution to correct these inequalities; and he censures the conditions in the existing system that tend to perpetuate the status quo. Because of this view, one would expect Dos Passos to denounce journalism as a contributing factor.

However, Dos Passos makes only an implied criticism of the newspaper. He uses some headlines and stories which he feels either fail to present the truth properly or flagrantly favor the opposition; he places the newspaper by implication squarely in the realm of big business; and he takes jibes at some practices commonly employed by newspapers in obtaining stories. Yet he never treats in any great detail the all-encompassing power of the newspaper in influencing public opinion, in using its editorial voice, or in molding the values, whether sound or questionable, held by the general citizenry.

Slightly more than three decades after The Big Money Dos Passos criticizes a phase of freedom of expression in The Great Days (1958). Herein he has Roger Thurloe, upon entering the armed services after the outbreak of World War II, tell Mortimer Price that he (Price) is needed as a journalist out of uniform to advise those in uniform of the real truth of the moment. The implication, of course, is that only the newspaper and magazine writer beyond the reach of the government can express himself without restraint. Also in this work, Dos Passos stresses, once again by implication, the important role of unfettered journalism in a democratic society.

In his use of newspapermen as characters, Dos Passos resorts to stereotypes. Jimmy Herf, for instance, one of the important characters in Manhattan Transfer (1925), worked as a newspaper reporter for an extended part of his life. Herf, however, is simply a commonly held conception of the newspaperman--a heavy drinker, a misfit, a man who spends his time hoping to fall into the right spot rather than working under a program of self-discipline to earn that position. In Jimmy Herf, therefore, Dos Passos merely depicts another newspaperman in the popular vein; he serves as one of a cast of characters created only to give a panoramic view of New York.

William Faulkner, like most other major writers of his time, does not deal with the American newspaper because it does not fall within his sphere of interest. As a beginning writer, he experienced difficulty in finding the material which he could handle best, and as a result, he experimented widely in form and subject matter. Later, it seems, he accepted the advice of Sherwood Anderson who told him that he must write of "that little patch of country" which he knew best. Thereafter, he settled down to probing for the deep inner meaning of life as he saw it reflected in his native

Mississippi. Using his own Oxford region, which he renames Yoknapatawpha County, he deals with people who rarely have any contact with the newspaper. Hence, he has no occasion to enter the world of journalism other than to obtain a minor character--as, for example, the newspaper editor who assists Gavin Stevens in Go Down, Moses (1942) to raise funds to bring home the body of Butch Beauchamp, the young negro executed for killing a Chicago policeman.

Also significant is the fact that Faulkner's fictional works deal essentially with a world of the imagination. Faulkner moves constantly away from the common experiences of existence to depict those familiar to the imbecile, such as Benjy in The Sound and the Fury (1929); to those of the social degenerates, such as the Snopeses who appear in so many of his works; and to those of the rascals, such as the Sutpens who move as the central characters in several of his major writings.

Ernest Hemingway produced novels before the 1930's--notably The Sun Also Rises (1926) - but he received his first really wide critical acclaim with A Farewell to Arms (1929) and the works which appeared in the next decade. Hence he is directly associated with the Thirties.

Hemingway--newspaperman, war correspondent, adventurer, and novelist--displays a rather narrow field of interest. He focuses on the physically vigorous man contesting against other men or the forces of nature; on the drama of the bull fight, the battle field, the tavern, and other places where men are likely to engage in dramatic combat; and on the struggles of the lost or the ill-adjusted person to find his place in society. In the words of Robert Penn Warren, Hemingway places great emphasis on "physicality,"[2] and like Robert Louis Stevenson, finds "his characteristic hero and characteristic story among the discards of society."[3]

Because of these interests, Hemingway never makes any full length considerations of institutions. Rather he centers his stories around the adventurer, the soldier, the physically maimed, the heavy drinker, and the depressed or otherwise disturbed personality as they struggle unsuccessfully in a world which they choose not to try to understand.

Hemingway, of course, knew the newspaper world, and like so many other writers, went to it for characters. But also, like so many others, he simply used the characters to round out a story. Thus we have Jake Barnes, the socially maladjusted and heavy drinking newspaperman who is the narrator in The Sun Also Rises; Karkov, the Russian correspondent in For Whom the Bell Tolls; and other characters who have little better than walk-on roles in other Hemingway novels. Thus Hemingway's newspapermen, one and all, are drawn almost completely as characters apart from the day to day activity of the working journalist.

Thomas Wolfe treats the newspaper world in several of his works, but because of his pre-occupation with people as individuals, he never sees the newspaper as an institution to be examined, analyzed, or interpreted. Rather, he enters the newspaper world only to depict an interesting character or to follow one whom he is already portraying. The fulcrum of his analysis is, of course, always philosophical. He constantly examines his characters in the light of their activities, their thoughts, and their personalities in order to explain the aura that envelopes their lives. Because of Wolfe's abiding interest in people and his ability to write graphically, he has depicted quite successfully certain types of newspaper personalities and atmospheres.

In Look Homeward Angel (1929), for example, the tragic Ben Gant works for The Citizen, a small Southern daily, in a position directly associated with the printing and the circulation of the paper. Herein Wolfe speaks affectionately and competently, as only someone who knows the lure of printing can, of the beauty of a well printed page, the precision of the presses, and the overall satisfaction derived by compositors and pressmen in viewing their handiwork. He speaks of the pleased reaction of Harry Tugman, the pressman, "casually scanning the warm pungent sheet" and exclaiming, "What a makeup!"[4]; and he speaks of the little print shop with its "good warm smell of ink and steel."[5] The satisfaction and general understanding of this particular atmosphere are, of course, beyond the comprehension of anyone who does not know printing.

Wolfe also displays a knowledge of two other phases of journalism in this work--the contempt which most newspapermen harbor for the "society" page (now more commonly known as the "womens" page) and the conflict which frequently exists, with an accompanying edginess, between the editorial and the mechanical departments of the newspaper.

As Harry Tugman and Ben Gant sit together in a local lunch room, Tugman goes to great lengths to ridicule "Little Maudie" and her column, "The Younger Set," by extemporizing an imaginary column filled with vulgarities and indecencies--all done in the form of a parody on the author's style and content. Wolfe's treatment of the conflict between editorial and mechanical departments is handled quickly but pointedly in Tugman's anecdote to Gant about ordering the editor, Jimmy Dean, out of the press-room by telling him "to take his little tail upstairs" to the editorial department where he "belongs." To Dean's resort to authority, "I'm the editor," Tugman gives one quick and terse reply: "I don't give a damn if you're the President's snotrag. If you want any paper today keep out of the press room."

Wolfe also captures quite capably the peculiar atmosphere of the small town newspaper office of the twenties and the thirties in The Hills Beyond (1935). This work, a collection of odd pieces which have only, at best, a distant relationship to one another, contains a pleasing selection in one-act play form entitled "Gentlemen of the Press." In this piece, several aspects of small town journalism are portrayed with a remarkable power of portraiture, a sensitivity, and a clear note of authenticity. There are the typical loud, affectionately abusive, bawdy exchanges between the working newspapermen; there is the omnipresent controversy, with all its positive and uncompromising judgments, regarding the nature of "good" newspaper writing; and there are two well drawn newspapermen types in Ted Willis and Red Tugman. Also, the Associated Press "office" within the editorial department and the composing room are presented with thoroughness and insight.

Thus Wolfe stands as a novelist who, among his other abilities, is able to reproduce the atmosphere of the small newspaper establishment with candor, understanding, and powers of portraiture.

James T. Farrell is often termed a "Proletarian" novelist because of a deep concern with the social issues of his time, especially as they exist in his native Chicago. He interprets these issues through Studs Lonigan, Danny O'Neill, and his other characters, all of whom move against an urban milieu.

By every rational conjecture, Farrell should have singled out the American newspaper for analysis. His unrelenting social probings and his career of part-time reporter should certainly have drawn his attention to the newspaper. In addition, his liberal political philosophy should have occasioned at least some denunciation of the conservative press. Yet Farrell stands as another novelist who should have attempted, but did not, to interpret the newspaper. Like so many others, he draws an occasional character from the newspaper world but he never attempts to probe the world, but itself.

II

Naturally, within this decade of the 1930's, many minor novelists produced works which achieved only a temporal recognition; that is to say, they were widely read but soon forgotten. In this group are many which touch upon newspaper journalism. For purposes of examination, they can be classified broadly as those which (1) treat one or more phases of editorial policy, (2) depict the newspaperman at work, and (3) merely use the newspaper world as a background.

Of the novels which treat one or more phases of editorial policy, exactly six merit consideration on the bases of extent of treatment and number of copies circulated. They are: Carl H. Claudy's _Girl Reporter_ (1930); Mildred Gilman's _Sob Sister_ (1931); Emile Henry Gauvreau's _Hot News_ (1931) and _The Scandal Monger_ (1932); Vincent Sheean's _The Tide_ (1933); and Phil L. Anderson's _Court House Square_ (1934).

Claudy's _Girl Reporter_ and Miss Gilman's _Sob Sister_ treat the same subject--the woman writer who points her material toward those interested in maudlin sentimentality. She is likely to write in a gushy and "tear jerking" manner of little tragedies, funerals, misfortunes, or anything else that can arouse an emotional response in the reader who makes little or no attempt to control emotions. In days past, this kind of writer was known as a "sob sister," a term made popular in large part by Miss Gilman's title. Currently, the term is used rarely, despite the presence of "sob sister" writing in many newspapers, especially the tabloids.

In Girl Reporter, Pat Prentiss, a millionaire's daughter, suddenly loses her fortune and is cast on the world to support herself as a reporter on the Times-Star. The story then concerns itself with her experiences, perils, and scoops as she moves through a role that entails a great deal of "sob sister" activity. In Sob Sister, Jane Ray, a hard boiled girl reporter who is outstandingly successful in her work, is troubled by the competition of Garry Webster, a reporter for a competing paper. As the story progresses she falls in love with Garry; she is kidnapped; and she is re-united with Garry, whom she eventually marries.

The importance of these two novels is that they present rather clearly a segment of the newspaper world which places a high value upon a morbid type of news in order to increase circulation. To the mature newspaper reader, the appeal of such material has always been an enigma. But for the readers of these books, the matter certainly assumes something of a new clarity.

Gauvreau's Hot News makes an examination of the basic nature of the tabloid. Although it is not especially well written, it moves at a fast pace as it brings into focus the behind-the-scenes action of the tabloid in fostering an unhealthy interest in sex, crime, and corruption--all with the open aim of increasing circulation. Any consideration of the obligation to raise society, it seems, merits no attention whatever.

In this novel, Gauvreau presents his attack in more moderate and more objective terms than is his general custom. This approach, coupled with a rather thorough examination of major tabloid practices, makes his novel rather effective in accomplishing its purpose.

The Scandal Monger, one of the most discussed novels on journalism of all time, is a cry of horror at the negative influence which a newspaper writer can exert. Ostensibly the account of the rise and fall of a New York tabloid columnist, the story has an unmistakable parallel to the career and activity of Walter Winchell, a writer who stands as a journalistic phenomenon. Winchell, at the height of his power, was one of the most influential voices of his age. Delving into anyone's privacy, courting libel suits with an open defiance, and displaying a fear of no one, he helped to shape the viewpoints of thousands of his fellow Americans as he expressed his thoughts tartly and finally on a variety of subjects, many of which were clearly beyond his depth.

The influence of such writers Gauvreau considers a genuinely serious menace; and he says so flatly in his Preface and by strong implication throughout the story. However, Gauvreau's arguments lose force because of the loud, vitriolic, alarmist manner of the book. One has the feeling that the author could have been more convincing had he chosen to display the restraint and dignity required of sound argument.

Nonetheless, this novel stands as an authentic and serious analysis of the negative influence which a widely read columnist can cast over a citizenry, in spite of the heat which generates from its pages.

Sheean's The Tide is a fairly successful attempt to satirize the practice of some newspapers of creating "news" by distorting facts or blowing up a personality beyond proper perspective. Menachen Hanotrzi, a Syrian Jew, is a passionately religious and humanitarian minded man visiting New York in behalf of his religious activity. Some newspapers, desperate for news, make a deliberate and repelling attempt to lead him to the slaughter of social aggrandizement. Hanotrzi, however, refuses to cooperate. For his stand, he is discredited by the papers and he subsequently leaves, saddened and bewildered, for his Middle East home where his real work and opportunity lie.

This novel, both well written and plausible, exhibits a clear knowledge of the lack of ethics which some newspapers demonstrate. Hanotrzi is sincere, honest, and dedicated, but because he will not accede to the dishonesty of the newspapers, he incurs their wrath, thereby falling a victim to their blackmail.

Although this novel handles capably a situation to be found in newspaper journalism, danger exists in the fact that the uninformed reader may over-estimate its incidence. While most tabloids and many sensationally minded newspapers of conventional format often employ such practices, the newspapers which command the respect of the upper intellectual levels consider such a practice patently unethical.

Anderson's Court House Square is a study in the importance and difficulty of assessing small town feeling regarding its newspaper. The central figure in this work is John Mason, editor of the Plainville Press, a rural community newspaper. Mason, a forward looking individual, champions the cause of commercial aviation editorially, and thereby gains the wrath of subscribers and advertisers. Revenue decreases, and the paper totters badly. Eventually, however, it is saved by Mason's college educated son and a slangy, aggressive newspaper woman, Jo Robinson, who together supply the journalistic qualities and the business acumen necessary for the paper to weather its storm.

Although this novel seldom rises above the level of adequate achievement, it does delineate capably the seriousness with which the small community is likely to view its newspaper. Editors of such papers, one soon learns, must be, journalistically speaking, tight rope walkers performing at very high altitudes, often in the strongest of winds.

The novels of this decade which depict the newspaperman at work run the gamut from poor to quite good. Of these works, eight are especially worth noting. They are: Gene Fowler's Trumpet in the Dust (1930); James S. Hart and Garret D. Byrnes' Scoop (1931); Rosalie M. Campbell's Headlines (1932); Silas Bent's Buchanan of the Press (1932); Royce Brier's Reach for the Moon (1934); Robert Van Gelden's Front Page Story (1937); Hugh B. Haddock's City Desk (1937); and Louise Andrus' Though Time Be Fleet (1937).

Fowler's Trumpet in the Dust is an especially perceptive account of the reaction which a newspaperman can feel to the news which he encounters. Gordon Dale, a top flight journalist, constantly seeks for the riddle of life in the heap of news that he handles daily. Because of his own troubled life, made more difficult by his love for Nada, he is ever at loose ends. And as he contemplates the news and the people who make news, he finds nothing approaching a solution.

This story is skillfully related; it reflects excellently chosen detail; and it exhibits a thorough knowledge of journalism. But above all, it is worth reading for Fowler's unusual grasp of the effect which "news" can have on the newspaperman. Dale does not merely assess events and people in terms of their value in making his newspaper more entertaining or readable. Instead, like the true newspaperman that he is, he thinks in terms of human values. He is interested in people as people--in their hopes, their desires, their disappointments, their ability to meet life successfully.

The importance of Hart and Byrnes' Scoop rests on its ability to portray a common newspaper atmosphere. The story unfolds the tale of Snakes Shiel, star reporter, who has been sentenced to ten days imprisonment for drunken driving. In jail, he learns of the practice of a dishonest judge in dealing off pardons for fees. Out of jail, he becomes the spearhead of his newspaper's campaign to right matters in the entire local government.

Although the work is, at times, almost offensively melodramatic, it is nonetheless quite readable. More important, however, this novel has a strong redeeming quality: it presents a clear and an authentic picture of the big city room in action--with all its bustle, competition, and strange brand of comraderie.

Miss Campbell's Headlines is important journalistically because of the success with which it brings into focus a disagreeable function which the working journalist must often perform, that of pressing someone for "news" at a moment when that person rightfully deserves privacy or sympathy. In this story, a main character learns from newspaper reporters that her husband has been arrested for the murder of the woman whom he has married bigamously. Thereafter, they pursue her for facts relentlessly.

The newspapermen who most often face this unpleasant aspect of journalism are the district men who must visit the homes of accident and other victims for pictures for the next edition; the reporter who must interview the next of kin after disasters involving loss of life (mine cave-ins, factory explosions, etc.); and the feature writer interviewing the close relatives of the person on trial for a serious crime.

Bent's _Buchanan of the Press_ presents a revealing picture of the big city reporter at work. This novel follows Luke Buchanan, star reporter of the St. Louis _Press_, as he moves through his professional and private life. In his professional life, he functions with the aplomb of the champion as a newsman; in his private life, he is given to drunkenness and loose living.

The strongest feature of this novel is unquestionably its competent and understanding grasp of the hectic pace of work on the metropolitan daily. The demands made upon Buchanan are great. He must always get the impossibly difficult story against an ever-descending deadline; and he must always get every fact right. These demands, along with many others, he always meets, only to falter badly in his private life.

Brier's _Reach for the Moon_ is interesting for the historical picture it presents. It is the story of Harper

Poole, a San Francisco reporter of the early 1900's, who falls in love with a banker's wife and thereby creates the usual three-way difficulties.

As the story moves forward, it provides an excellent retrospective view of the newspaper office, the reporter, and the editorial department of the time. The author, writing from the vantage point of three decades later, has a basis for comparison obviously impossible for a contemporary. Thus he speaks understandably of the slower means of transportation, the limited means of communication, the older methods of composition and printing, and similar basic feature of preparing and printing the newspaper. This understanding, coupled with the author's competence, make this novel rewarding reading for anyone interested in the newspaper of that particular time.

Van Gelden's _Front Page Story_ has a limited significance as a presentation of the manner in which the newspaperman often works with the police. The story turns on the activity of a cub reporter who stumbles on a major clue of a mystery which he is covering, thereby earning from the police the sole rights to material for a front page story.

In presenting his story, Van Gelden, a former _New York Times_ reporter, displays his professional newspaperman's knowledge of the manner in which the newspaperman and the police "cooperate." The newspaperman often finds himself squarely dependent upon the police for essential information; and policemen often benefit from the help of the newspaperman. A favorable mention of a patrolman's name in a news story, for example, may not only boost that patrolman's ego, but may also aid in a promotion. Hence the newspaperman must know how to establish the delicate, understood relationships by which journalist and police work together.

Haddock's City Desk is an interesting, if superficial, story which has one revealing journalistic insight--the settled conviction that the newspaper world is a man's world. Bruce Carter, writer and editor, harbors the widespread prejudice against women in the newspaper world. He allows for the presence of women to handle the women's page and similar undertakings, but even then, his recognition is grudging. However, Carter makes an exception and a mistake. He hires an attractive woman with whom he soon falls in love, thereby bringing down upon himself severe domestic strife.

Miss Andrus' Though Time Be Fleet is important as a rather limited picture of the woman journalist at work. Marcia Ellsworth, the central character, is a successful newspaper woman because she has an almost unerring sense of that which makes interesting reading for women. Consequently, this story represents profitable reading on that count, even though it is a routine performance otherwise.

The novels of this decade which merely use the newspaper world for a background rather than attempt any interpretation of journalism are surprisingly numerous. A discussion of the most widely read follows.

John C. Mellett's Ink (1930) is another novel in the tradition of Booth Tarkington's The Gentleman from Indiana. Arthur Morton, a financially beaten young man, somehow gains the funds to buy a newspaper and immediately launches an editorial battle against corruption in his town of Columbia. In the course of events, he meets many obstacles before finally achieving success; yet he remains undaunted throughout.

The story is, at times, seriously distorted. It also becomes melodramatic and even flamboyant. Yet Morton is often quite convincing in his grasp of journalistic matters, thereby saving the narrative flow from grinding to a halt. In the main, however, this work has little to recommend it as an enduring creation.

Lloyd C. Douglas' Forgive Us Our Trespasses (1932) has as its main character Dinny Brumm, who becomes a successful writer of cynical journalism through his hatred of environment, family, and conventional religion.

Dinny's outlook on life and general philosophy leads to the loss of the girl he loves and a sinking deeper and deeper into his cynicism. However, through the chance discovery of a letter among his deceased mother's possessions, he changes his attitude and becomes a different and more emotionally stable person.

Brumm is drawn quite effectively as a person but as a newspaperman, he is nothing unusual. Therefore, this novel offers little as an endeavor touching upon the institution of journalism.

Rain on the Roof (1932), by Kay Lipke, is the stock triangle placed against a newspaper setting. Patty McBride loves Lance Randolph, a newspaperman. He, however, marries Patty's friend Joyce, only to desert Joyce and their infant because of a misunderstanding. Patty then displays a novel strain by shouldering the responsibility of supporting both Joyce and the child.

Henry J. Smith's Young Phillips (1933) is the story of a cub reporter who exposes and destroys a political machine run by gangsters. Although the book employs a newspaperman as its motivating force, it is still basically an adventure story rather than a newspaper story.

Graham M. Dean's Jim of the Press (1933) is nothing more than a boy's story with slight overtones of a mature novel. The author unfolds the story of a boy who, through perseverance and hard work, rises from helper in the linotype department to reporter to correspondent in the state capital. As an in-depth treatment of the world of the newspaper or the character of a boy, this novel lacks any special distinction.

Elliott Arnold's Two Loves (1934) is another story of a hard drinking, hard living, hard loving newspaperman. The world of newspaper journalism is drawn clearly but often superficially as the central character, Ted Hughes, lives through adventure after adventure. In essence, this novel is little more than routine performance. It lacks any real distinction as a story or an interpretation of any aspect of journalism.

Don Tracy's Round Trip (1934) is a straight, blunt, factual treatment of a man who begins his early youth as a failure, rises to great success as a newspaperman, and then, unable to withstand the shock of losing his wife and baby, falls back into a life of inebriety and eventual failure. It is, in short, an account of a journey from the gutter to the gutter.

Although this novel reflects a sound knowledge of journalism, it never goes far below the surface of newspaper atmospheres and practices. Hence it has, at best, a limited significance in this respect.

Kathleen Shepard's I Will Be Faithful (1934) relates the experiences of a girl who rises above family objections and control to become a newspaper woman. After a somewhat difficult start, she achieves considerable success as a writer and, in the process, acquires a newspaperman for a husband.

The most startling fact about this book is its wide sale. The most logical explanation is that Miss Shepard already had a following among women readers who purchased copies for the love story recounted herein.

Gertrude E. Mallette's *Private Props* (1937) appeals most directly to the adolescent girl reader. It concerns the activities of Lynn Carter, 19, who enters journalism by way of a small town newspaper in order to support herself and an aged housekeeper. In the course of her work, she relies on two props, courage and independence, to emerge, as expected, a winner on every count.

The strongest attribute of this novel is the sure touch which the author displays concerning the role of the woman writer on the small town paper.

Joseph Berger's *Copy Boy* (1938) and Adam Allen's *Printer's Devil* (1939) turn on the activities of adolescent boys in the newspaper world. *Copy Boy* centers about a youth who obtains a position of copy boy, from which he eventually rises to the role of reporter; *Printer's Devil* tells the story of Bob Wilson, a 12 year old, who works as a helper for one summer in the composing room of a country newspaper.

Copy Boy has nothing special to recommend it, even though the author's portrayal of journalistic matters is both sound and authentic. *Printer's Devil*, however, has an unusual quality: it depicts with a high degree of success the subtle appeal which the composing room has for anyone interested in printing. Through the senses of Bob Wilson, one learns considerable about the strange fascination which type beds and presses so often exert.

III

During the decade 1940-50, the primary concern of the citizenry of the nation was war. The decade opened with a realization of impending participation in a war, and the nation subsequently lived through four years of actual war (1941-45); the decade closed with the Korean Conflict in full momentum. It is not surprising, therefore, that the attention of most literary artists was naturally directed toward the tensions, the anxieties, and the questionings which such an atmosphere produces. Nonetheless, many novelists of this period produced works dealing with some facet of newspaper journalism.

Of these writers, however, none can be accorded front-rank status; that is to say, there were among them no Henry Jameses, Mark Twains, or William Faulkners. They were, for the most part, writers whose fame was both slight and short lived. A discussion of their writings on journalism within this decade follows. For purposes of analysis, these novels can be classified under the heading of those dealing with matters of editorial policy, those treating the newspaperman at work, and those merely using the newspaper world for backdrop.

Those dealing with matters of editorial policy are Kathryn White's Miss Stanton of the Cryer (1941), Ayn Rand's The Fountainhead (1943), and John Brooks' Big Wheel (1949).

Miss Stanton of the Cryer is the story of a young woman who, upon inheriting from her father a newspaper with a reputation for yellow journalism, resolves to change the image of the paper. Although she faces formidable obstacles, she eventually succeeds in attaining her goal, but not before learning how seriously she has underestimated the magnitude of her task.

Any competent critic could not miss the structural and interpretational weaknesses of this novel. Most noticeably, the tempo is uneven, and the characters lack genuine depth of portrayal. Yet this same critic would have to concede the author's realistic grasp of the problems inherent in changing editorial policy.

In The Fountainhead, Miss Rand comes quite close to an effective interpretation of newspaper journalism as she portrays Gail Wynand and his world. Wynand, a successful publisher, is efficient, demanding, over-bearing, and cynical; he is a man who has risen by conquering severe obstacles, by holding steadfastly to his hard beliefs, by viewing life as a long, rough road where assailants may leap from dark recesses to rob, to injure, or to kill. His world is largely of his own making. He fraternizes with no one, living his life according to his own firmly established philosophy.

Wynand is clearly molded in Miss Rand's objectivism. He lives, thinks, loves, and loses his grip on life in a purely mechanical manner. Yet as a publisher, he is an accurate and well drawn representation of personal journalism. He strives to gauge public taste and to cater to it; but he also attempts to change it. Thus his newspaper, The Banner, points toward satisfying reader demands while presenting material which Wynand thinks the public needs. Like many famous journalists, he resorts to unusual tactics to keep his staff in line. On one occasion, for example, he brings into the office a colorless, run-of-the-mill citizen and introduces him all around. Later, when the man has departed, Wynand explains his purpose: he wants to show the staff the kind of person for whom they are producing a newspaper.

Wynand further typifies a kind of heavy handed, confident control. He excludes material from print which he adjudges "crap"; he blue pencils anybody's stories at will, without explanation; he simply announces drastic changes; and he writes editorials without advice.

He, of course, does not command unreserved respect. Ellsworth Toohey, the only man able to speak bluntly to him, challenges his judgment frequently. Michael Layton declares behind his back that he "could teach him a thing or two about journalism," while his staff often accepts his judgments with the silent dissent that constitutes a reproof.

In portraying Wynand and his activities, Miss Rand sees quite clearly the inherent danger in the existence of the powerful publisher. Wynand is always in a position to influence the conclusions of his readers, to promote a cause, or to discredit a laudatory endeavor. He always has at his fingertips a powerful instrument for good or evil.

As one reads this book, he is struck by the obvious parallel to the lives of several powerful publishers such as Hearst and Pulitzer. Yet to prove that Miss Rand had a specific individual in mind would be difficult--and relatively unimportant. The important fact is that such a figure as Wynand can be present in our society.

Big Wheel concerns itself with one of the most subtle but important questions in journalism: to what extent do writers and editors believe in the material which they prepare for readers? This question, which naturally has numerous ramifications, is more provocative than answerable. Yet every journalist must answer this question constantly, and from his answer, he derives a significant part of his working philosophy.

Brooks focuses attention on the question rather than attempting to give a final analysis. Nonetheless, his central character and his lesser figures clearly reflect the conviction that the institution of newspaper journalism is highly significant, that one must realize his responsibilities therein if he is to fill his role properly, and that one's moral success as a newspaperman is in direct proportion to the soundness of his answer to the central question raised in this novel.

The four novels of this decade which treat the newspaperman and his work are George M. Hillman's _Fortune's Cup_ (1941); Robert St. John's _It's Always Tomorrow_ (1944); Alexander C. Sedgwick's _Tell Sparta_ (1945); and Clyde B. Davis' _Stars Incline_ (1946).

Fortune's Cup is a warmly and affectionaly recounted story of the quest for understanding between a father and a son. Larry Evans, a newspaper dramatic critic, faces the task of helping his son, Stan, who has just been expelled from college, to find himself and to establish a rapport with his father. To handle the problem, Larry obtains a job as reporter for Stan on his own paper; and thus Stan is cast into the whirl, the personalities, and the cross-fire of the city room.

Strangely enough, this background and atmosphere present the perfect setting for Stan and his problem. Eventually, he comes to a wholesome appreciation of his job, his father, and the world in general.

A genuine significance of this book may well escape the

casual reader: it is that the atmosphere of the newspaper world can have, and often does have, a therapeutic effect on the people therein. Newspapermen, brought face to face with all facets of life, generally tend to make a straightforward and objective examination of the people and events that make "news." Hence they often are able to place in proper perspective the fluctuations in human behavior that disturb so many other people.

It's Always Tomorrow (1944) and Tell Sparta (1945) are typical of the many novels appearing during the World War II years employing the foreign correspondent as a central character. Generally, the correspondent is used merely to observe the actions and the atmosphere of war-torn Europe, while at other times he is used in a more complex manner.

It's Always Tomorrow is actually a story of adventure and suspense. As World War II breaks out, the main character, having remained at his post despite threatening circumstances, finds himself trapped in Poland in the midst of the Nazi onslaught and subsequent occupation. However, after a series of dangerous and close escapes, he makes his way to safety by way of Budapest, Paris, and Bucharest.

The appeal of this book is largely historical. St. John, himself an experienced newspaperman, has presented a readable and authentic account of the problems of the correspondent in the strife-ravaged Europe of World War II. For the person interested in this aspect of the war, St. John's novel can serve as edifying reading.

Tell Sparta represents a more extensive use of the correspondent. It is, in essence, the story of five correspondents--three men and two women--as they move about

Europe in quest of big stories. Although the novel is ostensibly a straight narrative, one cannot miss its satirical vein. Sedgwick believes that some correspondents serve dishonestly the people of whom they write by sacrificing objective reporting to sensationalism. Even more important to Sedgwick, however, is his conviction that the correspondents forsook the Greek people during their dark days of the early 1940's. The behavior of the five correspondents makes this point for him.

The importance of Tell Sparta lies in the question which it raises regarding the integrity of the foreign correspondent. As a work of art, it is little more than fair.

Clyde B. Davis' Stars Incline (1946) is the story of Barney Morgan, a newspaperman who moves from Denver to New York to the Europe of World War II. Davis, a professional newspaperman, has succeeded rather well in explaining a reaction of many seasoned journalists: it is the feeling that home is wherever one is doing his work. Hence many professional newspapermen, like many armed services career men, adapt themselves readily to whatever area their careers may take them.

IV

Of the novels which merely use the newspaper world as a backdrop, none rises above the level of adequate achievement.

Lucile S. Edgerton's In Walked Anny (1940) is the story of a farm girl who comes to the big city to work as a reporter. In the course of her work, she meets gangsters and pursues the expected exciting and dangerous road thereafter. Naturally, all ends well.

Emma Bugbee's Peggy Covers the Clipper (1942) is simply another story in Miss Bugbee's "Peggy" stories. Peggy now has a husband, Peter McFarland, and she is a newspaper woman with a special mission. Her job is to write stories extolling the ideals of womanhood. In executing her assignment, she concentrates on the arrivals and departures of the Clipper, the famous air flight of the late thirties and early forties, where she interviews a wide variety of famous women. Although the knowledge of journalistic procedures is sound, the book is, at best, interesting only in spots.

Charles H. Hoffman's Somewhere I'll Find You (1941) is the story of two brothers who are top flight reporters. As newspapermen, they have occasion to travel all over the world to cover wars, but unlike most newspapermen in such circumstances, they always live in luxurious accommodations.

This novel is exciting and, at times, captivating in dramatic interest. In no sense, however, is it genuinely unusual, even though it demonstrates a thorough knowledge of the work of the newspaperman pursuing a war.

Len Zinberg's Hold With the Hares (1948) chronicles the period between 1932 and 1945 in the life of Steve Anderson, a newspaperman with low moral standards and a basic instability. Anderson, however, eventually sees his errors and sets out to improve. This novel has no significance journalistically because once again there is only a light and superficial treatment of the newspaper world.

Paul Wellman's The Chain (1949) is the first of two novels in which he uses the newspaper world as a background force. Herein a crusading episcopal minister in Jericho, Kansas, has to undergo a series of difficult experiences to discharge his responsibilities as a clergyman and as an agent for civic improvement. Finally, he loses his life at the hands of a mob incited by the local newspaper's disclosure of a dark chapter in his past life.

The only journalistic significance of this novel lies in its raising of an old question of editorial policy: what guidelines should a newspaper establish for printing harmful information?

Notes

1. This fact is also surprising because of Dos Passos' almost obsessive interest in institutions. Critic Michael Millgate says of him, "Dos Passos has always been preoccupied with institutions . . . In his novels, from the army world of Three Soldiers to the bureaucratic Washington of The Grand Design, he has continually depicted man in his relation to the institutions which alter, condition, and control his life . . . ." (See American Social Fiction, Oliver & Boyd, Edinburgh and London, 1964, p. 142.)
2. "Why Do We Read Fiction?", Saturday Evening Post, 1962.
3. Introduction to A Farewell to Arms, Charles Scribner's Sons, New York, 1949.
4. Charles Scribner's Sons, New York, 1929, p. 168.
5. Ibid., p. 535.
6. Ibid., p. 170.
7. The second is Jericho's Daughters (1956), a story of marital discord. In this work, Mary Agnes uses her husband's newspaper as a tool against his infidelity and the blackmail with which she is threatened.

Chapter 4

The Newspaper in the Novel, 1950-69

I

Of the novelists of the period 1950 to the present, the two most often designated as "important" are Norman Mailer (1923-) and Saul Bellow (1915-). Each has done at least one widely acclaimed book, and each has shown flashes of talent usually associated with "major" novelists. Mailer and Bellow, for the most part, consider important issues of the immediate present, even though they concentrate principally on the deep and troubling questions of all time. Their focus is on character depictions, difficulties faced by individuals, and philosophical questions. Neither of them ever analyzes institutions in detail.

As a novelist, Mailer has won the respect of critics, in varying degrees, for four works: _The Naked and the Dead_ (1948), _Barbary Shore_ (1951), _The Deer Park_ (1955), and _An American Dream_ (1965). _The Naked and the Dead,_ generally acknowledged as Mailer's greatest claim to a lasting reputation, is a story of World War II wherein the struggles of the main characters, both officers and enlisted men, against the army and against nature are depicted. His _Barbary Shore,_ which centers about a rooming house in Brooklyn Heights, abounds in overtones of leftist political questions, a denunciation of the present political structure of the United States, and a clear call for corrective action. Yet the essential purpose of the novel is not quite clear. Mailer has constructed an allegory, but the allegory is opaque. The Deer Park is another analysis of society, as Mailer sees it, with all its false values, conflicts, and shaky moral standards, set against the chrome, the stucco, and the neon lights of Hollywood, California. An American Dream is a recounting of a thirty-two hour sojourn of Stephen Richard Rojack, a war hero, college teacher, and television performer in the New York area. Rojack, like so many of Mailer's other characters, is trying to find the essence of life by living a series of bizarre and often frightening experiences.

In these four works, Mailer evidences a genuine interest in the problems faced by the citizenry of the present--as well as an interest in social and political questions generally. Critic Norman Podhoretz says of Mailer that "his work has responded to the largest problems of this period with a directness and an assurance that we rarely find in the novels of his contemporaries."[1] Yet his interest does not include the newspaper. When mentioned at all, as for example, in Barbary Shore, it is merely catalogued as part of the general scene; it is simply a small item in a large setting.[2]

Bellow, like Mailer, is clearly a novelist of his time and place in approach and subject matter, even though he may set his scene in Africa as he does in Henderson the Rain King. His characters move against a contemporary background, they face the problems of the present, and they succeed only when they adjust to the life about them. Marcus Klien's judgment is typical of that of most critics. He sees Bellow's main characters as part of the "alienation to accomodation" journey enunciated by David Reisman in explaining the 1950's. The characters, finding themselves uncomfortable in their estrangement from society, proceed to adjust accordingly. They "face problems which are reducible to a single problem: to meet with a strong sense of self the sacrifice of self demanded by social circumstances."[3]

Whether the character is Augie March, Tommy Wilhelm, or Henderson, he faces a society wherein problems are encountered, struggles are inevitable, and some bending (adjustment) is demanded. When this bending is accomplished, a more comfortable life ensues; and that is precisely the course chosen by the characters.

Like Mailer, Bellow does not treat institutions in his novels. His rare mention of newspapers, as in _The Adventures of Augie March,_ are merely routine citations; they are never interpretations.

Mailer and Bellow seem to feel that the novel is the place for the interpretation of character--especially the character who finds himself apart from society or the mainstream of popular judgment--while they seem to feel that other forms of prose should serve for direct evaluation and criticism of society. Mailer, for example, has unleashed a strong opinion against the official foreign policy of the United States in his _Viet Nam_ (1967), an out-and-out diatribe. Bellow has made direct judgments on American society in essays prepared in his role of fellow of the Committee of Social Thought, University of Chicago.

II

Of the novelists of this period who rank favorably with Mailer and Bellow, none has elected to handle extensively the institution of newspaper journalism. There are writers like Carson McCullers and William Styron who fasten their attention principally on the eternal conflicts of the soul as found in a distinctly local setting. There are writers like Truman Capote and John Steinbeck who examine these same conflicts in more dramatic settings. And there are writers like Ralph Ellison and James Baldwin who concentrate mainly on the problems found within a specific ethnic group. Yet while all are undoubtedly aware of the newspaper, none treats it as anything more than a prop on a stage.

An example of this situation is Bernard Malamud, who has published three fairly important novels and a collection of short stories. Malamud is preoccupied with an analysis of the sad, the melancholy, and the alienated as they live out their existences in a society that is little short of hostile. Of his novels, the best on an American subject is _The Assistant_ (1957).[4] It is the story of Frank Alpine, an Italian, who robs Morris Bober, a Jewish grocer, and then tries to atone by helping Bober in the store without recompense. In the process, Alpine merely adds to his woes, eventually bringing on his own doom.

Because Malamud treats the lonely lot of the unfortunate and the maladjusted, he considers only those elements of background which bear on their situation. He views the newspaper and other institutions as parts of the physical world wherein he moves his characters and therefore gives them no interpretation apart from their relationship to individual characters. In fact, the newspaper is hardly more than alluded to--as in _The Natural_ (1952) where Roy Hobbs, the central figure, hears his disgrace shouted blatantly by newsboys on the street corners. Hobbs, a great major league pitcher who has agreed to "throw" a game, relents too late.

When the game is lost, Hobbs suffers infinite remorse and slinks about in burning shame. Malamud seems to be saying that newspaper publicity is a savagely cruel procedure; yet he says so only by implication, not by direct statement.

III

Naturally, during this period, many novelists of less than front-rank status produced works treating some aspect of newspaper journalism. As is to be expected, they focused their attention on many of the older concerns of editorial policy, but they also turned to some questions not treated heretofore. The following discussion treats the most significant of these novels. For purposes of analysis, they are placed under the headings of those dealing with (1) editorial policy matters, (2) columnists, (3) wire services, (4) the newspaperman at work, (5) the newspaperman as a routine character.

The novels dealing with editorial policy are (1) _The Prosecutor_ (1956) by Bernard Botein, _The Heartless Light_ (1961) by Gerald Green, _The Fools of Time_ (1962) by William E. Barrett, _A Certain Evil_ (1965) by David Kraslow and Robert S. Boyd, _A Kind of Treason_ (1966) by Robert Elegant, _The Seat of Power_ (1966) by James T. Horan, and _The Monument_ (1966) by Nathaniel Benchley.

The Prosecutor is the story of Edgar Bailey, an unscrupulous district attorney who wins an impressive array of convictions by rigging evidence and cases. The importance of this novel as a treatment of newspaper journalism lies in its portrayal of Bailey's techniques and successes in deceiving the newspapers. By strong implication the author raises two questions: Should a really competent newspaperman ever be deceived by a man like Bailey? What procedures should the newspaper follow to check on such officials as the district attorney? Although the author gives no full answers, he makes quite clear his conclusion that the questions are viewed much too lightly in every quarter.

The Heartless Light brings to center stage one of the most troubling aspects of newspaper journalism: the harm that the newspaper, as well as radio and television, can inflict on the person in the news.

This story centers on the distraught parents of Amy Andruss, a four-year old kidnapped from her Los Angeles home, as they face the merciless attention of reporters. The police have already bungled the case, and now the parents must suffer more stress from the "heartless light" of journalists striving to satisfy the ghoulish interests of the newspaper reader.

Clearly, there can be no quick answer to the question posed by this novel: Where does one draw the line beyond which the reporter does not pursue news? On the one hand, a minimal amount of common sympathy would grant an immunity from reporters to people who, like the Andrusses, are in the midst of overwhelming anxieties. On the other hand, the journalist has a job to do, regardless of his personal reaction to the immediate situation. And there the matter must rest.

The importance of this novel is that it places this problem, in all its ugliness, squarely before the reader. He may shy away from it, but at least he has seen it.

The Fools of Time employs an old device of the imagination to examine the obligation of the media of mass communication to report important developments despite Federal government opposition.

In this novel, the central character, a scientist subsidized in part by Federal funds, seeks a cure for cancer. As he proceeds, he suddenly discovers a serum that halts the aging process. Because of the heavy interest and the accompanying heavy control of the government in the field of science, however, he is unable to inform the world of the facts. This situation leads, in turn, to an examination of the role of mass communication in performing its basic purpose of communicating. The scientist feels that the media have an inescapable obligation to enlighten the populace on all matters pertinent to their welfare, and he also feels that the media have a heavy responsibility to guide men to intelligent decisions. In this instance, the author implies that the media are shirking their duties.

A Certain Evil is interesting for the question which it leaves in the mind of the reader: does the situation presented herein represent a common practice? In this novel, the main character is Joseph Warrick, a reporter who is requested by the State Department to aid in the overthrow of a Latin American dictator. Warrick is to write a strong story about a speech by the President of the United States which disparages the dictator, thus helping to discredit the dictator in the eyes of his nation.

Such collusion between small local governments and newspapers is known to be a common practice; and it has been suspected, with considerable substance, on the large municipal and state level as well, However, for it to exist on the national level is somewhat frightening. One wonders, for example, what the newspaperman is to receive as a reward for his "cooperation."

A further implication of this question concerns the

power which an individual newspaperman can wield. For one journalist to be in a position to aid significantly in the overthrow of a government is, to say the least, a startling thought. And the more one reflects, the more he finds far-reaching implications.

A Kind of Treason revolves about a situation which has recently caused considerable discussion in and out of official Washington, the activities of the Central Intelligence Agency. In this story, a correspondent is sent by his newspaper to Viet Nam to obtain the true facts of the bewildering conflict of the mid 1960's. At the same time, he operates in a sub rosa fashion to accomplish the same purpose for the C.I.A.

The author poses by implication an important question for journalists and society in general. He wants to know if the C.I.A., an organization whose Frankenstein qualities have been clearly exhibited, has used or is using the newspaper as an accessory. Hence he is raising a question that involves significantly the whole place and purpose of the newspaper and the newspaperman in society.

The Seat of Power tells of Duke Malloy, a reporter who obtains from an underworld character a story which reveals a conspiracy between the underworld and high municipal figures. Using this story as a springboard, Duke then proceeds to expose other municipal corruption and wrongdoing.

In addition to the interest of the narrative element, this novel is strong in its grasp of the power which the newspaper can exert as watchdog and investigator to insure sound local government. The author displays a practical knowledge of techniques and a firm understanding of editorial policy matters as he moves Duke through his daily work.

The Monument is another of the many treatments of a determined editor and the power of the press generally. A group in the New England town of Hawley has decided to erect a monument to the memory of one of its citizens killed in the Korean conflict. Another group, however, of which Rufus Goodman, editor of The Peninsula Gazette, is a leader, opposes the idea; and in the course of the ensuing action, Goodman makes his power felt.

Although Benchley's treatment is basically light, the book still enunciates rather clearly the inherent danger in a press that is not properly directed. The work also seems to underscore the importance of careful deliberation in taking editorial policy positions.

The four novels of this period which deal with newspaper columnists are, generally speaking, interesting but lacking in depth of thought and characterization. They are Richard L. Mealand's First Person (1950), Richard Condon's Some Angry Angel (1960), Edward E. Tanner's Love and Mrs. Sargent (1961), and Allen Drury's Capable of Honor (1966).[5]

First Person is a satirical treatment of newspaper columnists and the methods which they employ. Mealand sees the columnist as a kind of dishonest peddler--as a man who collects material illegally and immorally and then distorts it as he may please. Although Mealand is sometimes quite humorous, he nonetheless exhibits an ill-will toward this species of working journalist. He sees the columnist, in the main, as a seriously negative influence within society.

Some Angry Angel is a strongly worded and strongly opinionated story of Dan Tiamat, a man who rises from the gutter to become a top-flight New York gossip columnist only to fall back to the gutter and to rise again, this second time as an advice-to-the-lovelorn columnist.[6]

Despite the acid-like opinions expressed, the author clearly discerns some of the evils of this kind of writer. Especially worth noting is his carefully constructed indictment of the influence which the columnist can cast on society, even though he often lacks the background and insight to make a particular judgment. The author is also quite convincing in his subtle and overt condemnations of newspaper sensationalism as a force in the daily life of the great masses.

Love and Mrs. Sargent is another treatment of the power of the columnist. The story attempts basically to analyze Shelia Sargent, an advice-to-the-lovelorn columnist for a Chicago paper, who becomes so self-centered and blind to her own faults that she is a menace to herself and her readers.

Although this novel seldom rises above the commonplace, it does delineate the danger of unrestrained writing. If Shelia and people like her can continue writing after losing control of their emotions, what dangers can be anticipated?

Capable of Honor is a novel which continues essentially in the vein of Drury's two earlier and widely read works, Advise and Consent and A Shade of Difference. In all three books, the central purpose is to exhibit the below surface facts of a condition fraught with unsuspected danger. In Advise and Consent, it is the true picture of the diplomatic service. In A Shade of Difference, it is the clashings of the white and Afro-Asians in the United Nations Assembly. In Capable of Honor, it is the power which a columnist of national stature can employ as a check on the major affairs of the nation. The main figure in this novel is Walter Dobius, a columnist who makes life very difficult for the President of the United States as he attempts to handle foreign policy.

Like so many other novelists who depict the columnist at work, Drury is concerned about power without accompanying insight and sense of responsibility. Hence he is genuinely alarmed that a man like Dobius can achieve such a vast influence.

Although Drury is both readable and essentially sound, he loses force because of his superficial treatment and his alarmist tone. He could have succeeded better, one feels, if he had probed more deeply and presented his case more calmly.

The two novels of this particular time which treat the subject of the wire services make a very serious charge; they challenge vigorously the fundamental integrity of the services themselves. The novels are _Wire God_ (1953) by Jack Guinn and Willard Haselbush, written under the pseudonym of Jack Willard, and _The Last One_ (1956) by Dion Henderson.

Wire God is ostensibly the story of a dark character who tricks, maneuvers, and lies his way from tank town telegrapher to head of the World Press Service. In actuality, however, it serves more to raise questions and to provoke thought regarding the possibility that the wire services fake and distort news.

In perusing this book, one finds himself wondering if the central character's attributes are those required of a successful head of a wire service. One also wonders if the dishonest practices exhibited are typical of the day-to-day operating procedures of the wire organizations. The questions are made especially pertinent by the obvious care with which the authors, both Denver newspapermen, have assembled and presented their material. Furthermore, the questions are made troublesome by the objectivity displayed throughout the entire novel.

The Last One exceeds Wire God as a dark picture of the wire services because it is more thoroughgoing in its condemnation. Here, a Pulitzer Prize winning reporter, who has been assigned for a one-week period to a mid-western city, comes upon numerous plots and intrigues, among which is an attempt to bribe a United States Senator.

In recounting his story, the author obviously strains to portray the editorial atmosphere of a major wire service, and the result is an unpleasant picture. This particular wire service is guilty of distortion, suppression, and outright manufacture of news; honesty as an ethical consideration is given short shrift. Whereas Wire God merely raises questions, this novel stands as a flat indictment.

The quality which detracts most from this book is its abusiveness. The charges are so strongly made and the general tone is so castigating that emotion seems sometimes to prevail over reason. One often has the feeling, for example, that the author believes that any truth in a wire service story is a pure accident.

The novels within this seventeen-year period that handle some phase of the newspaperman and his work are especially interesting. Many interpret their subjects in an unusually capable and revealing manner, while several others, despite structural or other technical shortcomings, present important messages graphically. The order in which these works will be discussed is as follows: Robert Sylvester's Second Oldest Profession (1950); Vern Sneider's A Pail of Oysters (1953); Charles Christian Wertenbaker's The Death of Kings (1954); Henry Hough Beetle's Lament for a City (1960); Charles Angoff's Between Day and Dark (1959); Richard Powell's Daily and Sunday (1964); Robert Daley's The Whole Truth (1967); Arthur Gordon's Reprisal (1950); Douglas Kiker's The Southerner (1957); Jay Milner's Incident at Ashton (1962); and Elliott Chaze's Tiger in the Honeysuckle (1965).

Second Oldest Profession is a strongly phrased treatment of the situation in which a newspaperman accedes to the wishes of his publisher against his own innate sense of right and wrong. Ned Gorse, a reporter on the New York Globe, begins his career as a high minded journalist with the announced intention of warring on vested interests. However, when his material first crosses his boss' desk, he is told to desist or face certain pressures that forestall any chance of personal advancement. To the disappointment of his friends and his wife, he capitulates; and thereby he becomes a loser to himself and to others, even though he achieves success in his office.

This novel presents in full perspective one of the oldest and most difficult problems faced by the newspaperman--the problem of choosing between one's ideals and one's opportunity to rise. In this novel, Gorse succumbs to material gain and consequently represents a type of casualty likely to occur in such instances.

A Pail of Oysters is an interesting account of a common experience for many newspapermen--the frustration felt when one is unable to aid an unfortunate person in the "news" being covered.[7] Ralph Barton is an idealistic young American newspaperman covering the island of Formosa, the base for the Chinese Nationalists since the Red takeover of China. In the course of his work, he becomes involved in the fate of three Formosans who are victims of a slavery system. Barton tries desperately to help all three but succeeds in aiding only one. The cruel climax comes as he watches the other two, a pretty young girl named Precious Jade and her brother, shot to death on false charges of espionage.

Barton's suffering is familiar to that of many newspapermen in many situations. Often the journalist must cover a trial where he feels some injustice is being done or a meeting in which he knows the principals are dishonest or a session where an educationally limited person is being victimized. To help the person involved, he can sometimes resort to a signed feature story, but often he must accept his defeat in silence as Barton has to do in this story.

The Death of Kings is a novel that deals competently with the intrigue, the rivalries, and the office politics commonly found in the editorial office of the weekly news magazine. This situation, however, is not restricted to that particular kind of publication; it is common to the entire world of journalism. Hence the scene could be most newspaper offices.

This novel is also especially effective in its treatment of the chain of events and the subtle maneuvering that sometimes lie behind the creation of a given editorial policy. Often a clique or a little group obtains control and wields its power in the manner of the military high command--firmly, positively, unhesitatingly. Meanwhile, it keeps a careful eye on the enemy in order to safeguard its position.

Another strength of this work is the clarity with which it exhibits the process by which a lofty editorial policy can become tainted by the realities of the everyday world in which the publication circulates, especially any contact it may maintain with political personages. This book presents clearly, in an all too obvious parallel between its characters and living personalities, the dangers that arise when journalists and political figures become closely associated.

The literary merit of this novel is definitely uneven. From a strong and convincing beginning, it moves through a complex series of events that occasion a structural weakness. Then it gathers speed to end in genuine excitement. Throughout all, nonetheless, the author displays an extensive grasp of his main area of attention which is the attempt of one person or group to dominate a journalistic enterprise while making the necessary compromises to keep the publication in the financial black.

Lament for a City is a perceptive study of the ideological conflicts that often arise in the mind of the newspaperman. The story revolves about the activities of Cornelius Tyler, who first came to Hindon, a small New England town, as a young reporter for the *Courier-Freeman*. In this role, he witnesses the changing face of the city with all the social, political, and other implications therein; and all that he sees he recounts with the clarity and forthrightness of expression of the best of newspapermen. Tyler is filled with high ideals and a lofty sense of the role of the newspaper in society, but as time passes, he lets his views become tempered with a note of disillusionment and stoicism.

Beetle's novel is well written and, for the most part, quite interesting. Yet it cannot be considered a great novel in any sense of the term. Although Tyler is well drawn, the supporting characters seldom rise beyond adequate depiction. The book is significant, however, for the author's ability to etch the essential character of the city and for his comprehension of the reporter and the editor as functioning parts of the total institution of newspaper journalism. Tyler, as the narrator of the story, displays an unusual ability to interpret the particular kind of news in which he is interested. He is also well worth hearing as he speaks of editorial policy, newspaper practices generally, and the force which the newspaper can be for the uplift or the degradation of society.

In one sense, the strength of this novel is also its weakness. The author, a Pulitzer Prize winner for his history of the American press, has written a work that exudes too much of the case study and not enough of the artistic creation. Hence the book is, on the one hand, a thoroughgoing explanation of a newspaperman and his work while, on the other, it is a trifle too factual and matter-of-fact in tone to excite aesthetic sensitivities.

Between Day and Dark is a well executed and convincing depiction of another kind of frustration sometimes felt by the newspaperman. David Polonsky, the central character, is the offspring of Russian immigrants living in the Boston of the 1920's. Deeply impressed by the urgency of world events, he launches out on a career as reporter on a local paper because he sees there an opportunity to aid in the improvement of civilization. On the newspaper staff, however, he soon feels thwarted by the deeply entrenched sense of convention and the tendency to move with rather than against the current of society. Hence he finds little chance to accomplish his purpose against such odds. On the whole, this book is well written, and it is certainly enlightening. Still it remains as another example of a competent but not a great interpretation of a phase of journalism.

Daily and Sunday, which is sub-titled a "Novel of Newspaper Power and Politics," is a sharply written and convincing depiction of a newspaper staff at work. Powell, a former newspaperman, builds his story around the idea of a paper which has experienced through death the loss of its able publisher, Dave Buckley. The Board of Directors of the paper, The Evening and Sunday Mail, must now decide whether to seek a replacement for Buckley or to sell the paper to a chain. In the course of events, the clashings of personalities and the crossings of purposes typical of such a situation come to the fore.

Powell's novel rings with authenticity. The circulation tricks which competing newspapers are likely to play on each other, the contempt of one newspaperman for the opinions of another, and the pressures of newspaper work are presented graphically. In addition, the characters are carefully drawn and their speech is recorded with an engaging fidelity to fact. Yet the novel simply does not rise to the level of outstanding work. The shortcoming is, basically, a lack of genuine depth. One feels that a first-class reporter is detailing every part of an interesting story; one feels that he is actually in the editorial office of The Mail; and one feels the atmosphere of the newspaper world at every turn. Yet the story always moves on the surface of events; it does not plumb the depths below. The author is a competent observer and a skillful and interesting narrator, but he is not a writer of unusual talent. Hence this book, despite its authenticity and its perceptive qualities, stands as only another well done novel about the newspaper world.

The Whole Truth is another picture of the American newspaperman abroad and his work. It recounts the thoughts and activities of Paul Pettibon, a front rank journalist and Pulitzer Prize winner who, as head of the Paris bureau of an American newspaper, comes into contact with Walter Ard, a young newspaperman of considerable promise. In casting the men side by side, the author gains the opportunity to analyze their characters and their philosophies through the element of contrast.

This work is especially interesting in its depiction of Pettibon's philosophy as a working journalist. He sees the vast significance of his function, but he is always acutely aware of the accompanying demands. Among other requisites, he must keep abreast of the entire history of contemporary France; he must strain constantly to locate the important stories; and meanwhile, he must check ceaselessly to insure the accuracy and the completeness which a front page story, such as his always are, requires. To meet these demands, Pettibon believes, one must forever stand in awe of the responsibility which is his.

The critical acclaim accorded The Whole Truth by professional newspapermen is well worth noting. In passing judgment on this novel, most journalists have found little to criticize adversely and much to praise. They are especially impressed by the manner in which the author delineates the underlying tensions experienced by the newspaperman who finds himself in conflict with editorial practices forced upon him. Because Pettibon is so keenly aware of his responsibility in presenting material to the reading public, he is genuinely troubled by the business attitude of owners and publishers which shoulders aside all sense of professional commitment.

Reprisal is the first of four novels within this period that deal with the working newspaperman and the civil rights struggle. A white reporter from the North, who serves as narrator of the story, gives his account of a struggle between blacks and whites in a Georgia community where four blacks have been killed by white men. Although the author strives for objectivity, his sympathy with the black community is quite clear.

The importance of this book is simply its effectiveness in telling the story through the eyes of a newspaperman. The author demonstrates a professional knowledge of how the reporter thinks and acts in this kind of situation.

The Southerner also uses the newspaperman as the medium to interpret a racial matter. Jess Witherow, a beginning reporter and native of Antioch, a Southern city, is assigned to cover the trial of Will Taylor, a black college teacher falsely accused of assaulting a high school principal. The pattern of the case is, of course, an old one. Community leaders have trumped up a charge in order to "keep the Negro in his place."

Witherow finds himself torn, as the newspaperman often does, between loyalties. He feels a deep affinity for his home town and all that it means to him, but as a conscionable young man, he clearly discerns the evil involved. In the end, his sense of honesty triumphs but only after a traumatic struggle.

Journalistically speaking, this book has merit as a depiction of the psychomachia which the newspaperman may suffer when covering events such as this trial. Otherwise, the novel does not especially rise.

Incident At Ashton concerns the story of a crusading editor and the civil rights disturbances. Ashton, a small Southern town, is determined to retain its standard of white supremacy. When a black man attempts to register to vote, he is turned away, and a few days later, his body is found in a nearby river. The local sheriff, who displays only the mildest of interest in the case, is then prodded by Phil Arrows, editor of the town's paper, into solving the case.

The strength of this novel lies in the author's firm knowledge of how a newspaper in such a situation as this can best accomplish its purpose by standing its ground quietly but firmly.

Tiger in the Honeysuckle depicts effectively the process by which a reporter can change his mind on racial questions by virtue of covering a certain type of story. Chris Haines, a reporter in the town of Catherine, Mississippi, is covering a Negro voter registration drive where he sees rank injustices committed. A segregationist by sympathy, he is appalled by the sordidness and the blatant anti-black activity to the extent of shifting his position. He is further influenced by the presence of Jonee Hamilton, a light skinned negro girl, for whom he experiences a strong attraction. With his change of conviction comes a change in his writing and the inevitable showdown with his publisher.

Once again, therefore, is an interesting but not exceptional novel that exhibits a realistic grasp of a phase of the newspaperman's life.

IV

The novels within this period which employ a newspaperman as a routine character are quite numerous. Sometimes, of course, he is drawn more extensively than others, but in the main, he seldom performs extensively as a newspaperman. The most widely read of these novels are discussed below.

Reynolds Packard's Kansas City Milkman (1950) simply uses the newspaper world as a background against which to etch two characters, Clay Brewster and Don Shelby, newspapermen living in Paris. The story is a light and unimportant treatment of their thoughts and philosophy of newspaper work presented in a manner designed to entertain.

Shriek With Pleasure (1950) by Toni Howard is the account of Carla MacMurphy, a foreign correspondent, as she experiences a variety of adventures and love affairs. Actually, there is little journalism in this work. It is, in essence, a light adventure story placed on the outer fringes of the world of journalism.

God's Men (1951) by Pearl S. Buck deals with the mind of a selfish publisher who owns a string of tabloids as opposed to that of a more humane, altruistic man of the same age. Both men are sons of missionaries to China, but there the similarity ends. William, the publisher, is aloof, disdainful, arrogant. Clem, the plain citizen, is kindly, solicitous, sympathetic. Miss Buck's thought appears to be that of analyzing the influence of early background on mature development.

In the course of this novel, the author attempts to handle the basic philosophy of newspaper journalism, but she never really examines any issue in depth. Hence her work remains nothing more than another surface treatment.

Come Fill the Cup (1953) by Harlan Ware is a rather unusual use of a newspaperman as a major character. He is a city editor who has accomplished the difficult step from inebriate to absolute teetotaler. However, this commendable reform spells trouble. His friends, his friends' wives, and people whom he scarcely knows press him to employ his good offices to reform the inebriate in their lives. Thus he undergoes daily a strain that tends to make him edgy.

Small World (1959) by Keith Wheeler is the love odyssey of Web Harmon and Sara Ingalls, foreign correspondents, from their first meeting in an army hospital in World War II Saipan to their re-uniting after a series of stormy events.

This novel, however, does have some merit as a treatment of journalism. The observations and philosophizing upon the world of the newspaper have an interesting and authentic ring.

Sun Is My Shadow (1960) by Robert Wilder is simply another instance of a novelist employing a newspaper man as the medium through which to tell a story. In this case, the function of the journalist is to recount the atmosphere of the United States between the late 1920's and the coming of World War II.

Race of Rebels (1960) by Andrew Tully tells of Michael Kane and Margaret Ames, newspaper reporters, who witness the rise of the Fidel Castro regime in Cuba. Classifying this work as a novel, however, is somewhat questionable. Its factual overtones and its air of objectivity tend to make it more of an autobiographical account of the adventures of its author who covered the Castro ascendency as a reporter for the Scripps-Howard chain.

Shall Do No Murder (1960) by Holmes M. Alexander is an out-and-out murder mystery which employs an editor as a main character. As the editor never moves as a working journalist, the book obviously has no significance in the area of journalism.

No Mother To Guide Her (1961) by Anita Loos is a pleasantly satirical treatment of Hollywood that employs two columnists. One sees all good; the other sees a thinly chromium plated society, presided over by shallow and cynical people. Although the book is interesting in places, it has little of a lasting quality about it.

They Walked Like Men (1962) by Clifford Simak uses the old device of the newspaperman-observer to recount a fantasy. Parker Graves, seasoned journalist, and his fellow citizens witness a series of strange happenings in their city. Buildings are bought up at fantastic rates, and leases on homes and apartments are not being renewed. Everywhere, people are becoming homeless and consequently desperate. Parker, armed with his newspaperman's zeal and investigative powers, goes after the facts.

After many strange and humorous experiences, he learns that a race from another planet have invaded the earth bent on exterminating the people here. Among other processes, they plan to achieve their goal by legal deprivation of shelter and food supply.

The significance of this book as a treatment of journalism is nil. It is no more than another story employing a newspaperman as a central character in order to utilize his skills in observation and investigation.

The Long White Night (1964) by Katherine Scherman unfolds the story of Douglas Ewen Michel, a young feature writer, who travels to the far North to do a series of articles on Eskimo life. Once there, he becomes so enamored of the civilization that he remains on to witness the change of season. Although Michel uses his journalistic background to seek facts and make deductions, the book does not touch on journalism as an institution.

The Empty Day (1965) by Richard Lockridge is basically a character study of newspaperman Martin Brent as a man rather than as a journalist. Hence the author concentrates on personality analysis and personal problems to explain Brent's difficulties. When, however, he does turn to Brent's activities as a reporter and later as an editor, he does display a competent knowledge of the newspaper world.

The Secret Swinger (1966) by Alan Harrington attempts to analyze the problems of George Pectin, a 43 year old newspaperman who loses his hold on life. As a result, he divorces his wife and leaves his job, only to learn, of course, that his problems remain with him because they are self-created. Although this work involves little of journalism, the author tries to show, with only a limited success, a correlation between newspaper work and the kind of disillusionment which Pectin experiences.

V

Some novels of this period which are treated in other parts of this book should be mentioned here in passing. Niven Busch's California Street, a character study of Anchylus Saxe, publisher, presents an interesting insight into the interweaving of the private and the professional life of the newspaper executive. Paul Gallico's Trial By Terror unfolds a perceptive account of the dangers sometimes experienced by the foreign correspondent. John Gunther's The Lost City is a vivid recounting of the newspaper correspondent circle of the Vienna of the early 1930's as well as an enlightening account of the behind-the-scenes thoughts of the intelligent and well informed foreign correspondent. Robert Nathan's Star in the Wind is a strikingly vivid portrayal of the emotional involvement which a newspaperman can experience in the news he covers. Peter De Vries' Comfort Me With Apples is a use of a newspaperman as a character moving principally outside the world of journalism, but in a sequel, Tents of Wickedness (1959), De Vries moves Chick Swallow into more journalistic activites, and he also uses Bulwinkle, editor and publisher of the Picayune Blade, as a central character. In this second novel, he also treats journalism more extensively by ridiculing pointedly the overconfidence, the unreasonable demands, and the general orneriness of disposition to be found among editors.

Notes

1. Introduction to Barbary Shore.
2. Mailer discusses quite pointedly the role of the newspaper drama critic in the introduction to Deer Park: A Play (1967). He feels that this particular critic wields an influence that can seriously threaten the whole institution of the theater.
3. Kenyon Review, XXIV (Spring, 1962), p. 203.
4. Critics generally rank his Pulitzer Prize winning The Fixer (1966) higher. The setting of The Fixer, however, is Czarist Russia. Therefore it has no pertinence for a study such as this.

5. No one of these novels can compare in depth of thought to Emile Henry Gauvreau's Scandal Monger.

6. An interesting comparison can be made between the central character is this work and the main figure in Nathanael West's Miss Lonelyhearts.

7. An interesting comparison can be made between this novel and Robert Nathan's A Star in the Wind.

Chapter 5

The Newspaperman in the Novel, 1900-69

I

The institution of American newspaper journalism has experienced some far-reaching changes in the twentieth century. Generally speaking, the newspaper has evolved from a comparatively small enterprise into a highly complex organization; from a publication handled by a small group to one divided into departments directed and staffed by specialists; and from a situation where many divergent voices created a healthy climate of differing opinions to one where the growth of chain ownership and the decreasing number of papers have fostered an all too apparent sameness from one paper to another. With these changes, there has naturally been an accompanying change in the creator of the newspaper--the newspaperman.

If one all-inclusive statement is to be made about the changes in the newspaperman, it is that he adjusted to the demands of his time; that is to say, as changes in the newspaper itself occurred, the newspaperman adopted new patterns of action, new attitudes, and new roles. Thus over the years, he has become something of another species even though he has always discharged his basic function of gathering, interpreting, and presenting "news."

To understand the changes in the newspaper world and the concurrent changes in the newspaperman, a grasp of two important phrases is necessary: they are "personal journalism" and "group journalism."

The phrase "personal journalism" covers the situation wherein one man, because of the nature of his position, is able to superimpose his personality on one or more sections of the newspaper. He may be publisher, top editor, or lesser editor; but he is so placed that he can make irrevocable decisions regarding editorial policy, make-up, content, or other salient features. His role is analogous to that of the captain of the whaler. He issues orders, changes course, and directs all activity as his personal judgment, re-inforced by experience, dictates. His underlings, like the crew of the whaler, come to know his personality and his abilities, and they follow his orders explicitly--whether they agree or not. Thus the whole activity reflects the strengths and the weaknesses, the considered judgments and the whims, the farsightedness and the shortsightedness of a personality; and it is successful in direct proportion to the ability of one person to make the right decision at the right time.

The term "personal journalism," however, has a second important meaning which is closely related to the first: it is used to designate the situation where the writer is placed on his own--as the feature story writer and the columnist so often are--to handle a given story as he may see fit.

In its first meaning discussed above, personal journalism is correctly associated with names like Richard Dana, Joseph Pulitzer, William Randolph Hearst, William Allen White, and the many others who, with varying degrees of skill and success, served as one-man command posts, guiding their papers through competition with other newspapers, changing reader tastes, and other situations which demand the constant attention of the newspaper which is to prosper. In its second meaning, personal journalism is to be associated with names like Henry L. Mencken, Stanley Walker, Heywood Broun, Walter Lippmann, and others who have always moved as individuals in their handling and interpretation of news rather than as representatives of an editorial policy committee.

Broadly speaking, personal journalism dominated the newspaper at the turn of the century and for the two decades thereafter before beginning to give way to group journalism in the late twenties. Personal journalism was the general practice at the turn of the century primarily because most of the newspapers were small. In fact, many of the small dailies in the rural areas had staffs of less than a half dozen to prepare and print the newspaper. Hence the man with the title of editor often did practically all the editorial work, and quite often assisted in make-up and printing as well. Because of the multi-faceted nature of his job, he had to be able to find news, to handle people, to write, and to analyze the reader interest of his community. Meanwhile, he had to possess the business acumen to keep his paper afloat financially.

In the instance of the larger newspaper of this time, specialized ability rather than versatility was demanded because these papers had staffs, much as they do now, for each department. They also had divisions within the departments (e.g., news, sports, drama, etc.) to handle details in a specialized manner. Yet even on these larger papers, personal journalism was common because the heavy competition between papers placed a premium on excellence and originality. Therefore, the newspaperman whose judgment and ability earned respect generally was placed in a position to make key decisions.

One can comprehend the nature of one kind of personal journalism by examining sound biographies of men like Joseph Pulitzer and William Randolph Hearst--men who dominated every phase of their newspapers' thoughts and activities. One can grasp the essence of another kind of personal journalism by reading the autobiographical works of men like Heywood Broun and Henry L. Mencken--men who were, above all else, independent thinkers.

A short and highly readable account of a phase of personal journalism is James Thurber's "Newspaperman".[1] Among other reminiscences, Thurber gives an excellent depiction of Norman (Gus) Kuehner, city editor of the Columbus (Ohio) Dispatch when Thurber broke in as a cub reporter in the summer of 1920.

Kuehner was the absolute monarch of the city room. He decided upon the events to be covered and the extent and nature of the treatment (he especially liked murder and other activities in which the police were involved, and he blew them up to the maximum of their dramatic possibilities); he ignored almost completely any women's news; and he constantly aired his contempt for college courses in journalism, sentimentality, and softness.

He further proclaimed his philosophy as a body of guiding principles for his staff, all of whom he controlled with a heavy hand and a finality of judgment. He was fond of quipping, "You get to be a newspaperman by being a newspaperman"; and he had a repertoire of sarcastic remarks to fit any situation in which some one dared disagree. In short, he considered the city room, purely and simply, as his personal domain, subject to him and him alone.

From an understanding of personal journalism, the meaning of "group journalism" becomes clear. It is the kind of journalism that results when major decisions become matters for group discussion; when editorial policy is controlled tightly by a designated committee; when all editors must work within a framework of established guidelines; and when, all in all, the entire newspaper structure resembles that of a large business house.

Under group journalism procedures, an editorial conference is generally held each day that the newspaper appears. These conferences, as one might assume, are gatherings of publisher (or his representative) and top editors to discuss the day's news, the successes and failures of recent editions, the editorial view to be taken on leading questions, and means of increasing circulation.[2] Thus a group makes the decisions made by individuals under the personal journalism structure, and the newspaper reflects a group, rather than a personal, kind of journalism.

The practice of group journalism has arisen fundamentally from the concept that in any large and complex structure --such as most newspapers now are--important matters are best handled through the deliberations and conclusions of competent groups.

As one examines the patterns of personal and group journalism as they are treated in the twentieth century American novel, one statement can be made immediately: every portrayal of a newspaper, a newspaperman, or a matter involving journalism has been treated only through the medium of personal journalism; there is no even remotely extensive treatment of group journalism. Therefore, as one examines the twentieth century American novelist's treatment of the newspaperman, he must think constantly in terms of personal journalism.

II

As the American novelist has portrayed the twentieth century American newspaperman, he has selected individuals from many corners of the newspaper world, he has given them a variety of personalities, and he has surrounded them with environments that range from extremely friendly to impossibly difficult. Further, he has allowed them everything from complete success as individuals and as newspapermen to unmitigated failure in these same areas.

Despite wide variations in portrayal, however, these newspapermen character creations can be placed for purposes of analysis and discussion under five headings.

The first type of newspaperman found in the twentieth century American novel is an individual whose quirks of personality render him unable or unwilling to adjust to the world about him; he is a man who cannot be or does not desire to be a part of the society wherein he must earn his living. As a result of his conclusions about life, he may be openly resentful or bitter, or he may choose to sulk in dreary solitude. He may be harshly vociferous in his condemnation of men and belligerently defiant in his physical attitudes, or he may have thrown up his hands in despair to live out his days in stoical silence. Whatever his fealing, he is squarely at odds with society and the world in general. Hence, for him the experiences of the working journalist usually serve to deepen a particular brand of misanthropy.

The most familiar example of this type is Eugene Witla, central character in Theodore Dreiser's The Genius (1915).[3] Witla, who yearns for a career as a painter but finds his path blocked by his own limitations and a society that gives little encouragement to artists, is a study in frustration, vacillation, and shallowness. Lacking steadfastness of purpose, he moves through a series of jobs and love affairs, blandly indifferent to any genuine sense of responsibility, either to people or to a moral code. His failure he attributes to the conditions of the world--never to himself. Throughout all, he remains the dissatisfied, grumbling individual, constantly demanding that upon which he can lay no proper claim.

Although Witla works in the newspaper world, leaves it, and returns as an advertising department employee, he is never a newspaperman in the real sense of the term. He never knows any thrill in seeing material placed in type. He never experiences any over-riding sense of the newspaperman's place in the destiny of the times. He never really feels the newspaper business in his blood. He is, in short, simply a traveler through the world of journalism, one who is not only ready but eager to depart.

A somewhat similar character is Jack Burden, a dominant figure in Robert Penn Warren's All the Kings Men (1945). In this story, which is cast against the backdrop of the late 1920's and the early 1930's, Burden is a faithless, homeless cynic who, as Warren tells us, leaves his position on The Chronicle because for him the newspaper world holds no idealistic significance. He sees his role only as the means to earn a living; he discerns nothing of the importance of journalism as an institution or of The Chronicle or any other newspaper as an influential element within society. The smell of printer's ink, the freshness of the newly printed page, the mustiness of the city room hold no lure. He moves simply as another figure in the workaday world.

Similar portrayals are Ernest Hemingway's Jake Barnes in The Sun Also Rises (1926), a somewhat confused and unstable individual wandering on the outer fringes of society in search of the answer to a more contented existence; Harvey Swado's Joe Burley in Out Went the Candle (1955), an unsteady young man who dreams of fame as a foreign correspondent while being restricted to covering "hen house fires and Rotary Club luncheons" until World War II takes over his life by making him a draftee; O'Mara, the main character in Laurence Greene's novel of the same name (1938), a tramp newspaperman who cannot control his tendency toward drunkenness long enough to employ properly his genuine talent; and many other newspapermen who make brief appearances to round out stories by other twentieth century American novelists.

One newspaperman character in this first category of the ill-adjusted merits special consideration because he has been widely accepted by the reading public as representative of the victimizing influence which newspaper work is sometimes thought to exert. He is the central character in the novel Miss Lonelyhearts (1933),[4] by Nathanael West (real name, Nathan Weinstein, 1903?-40); and he is a weak, almost psychopathic man who never maintains any genuine grip on life. Because he writes the advice-to-the-lovelorn column for a New York newspaper under the pseudonym of "Miss Lonelyhearts," he is known by that name alone.

This novel is essentially a depiction of Miss Lonelyhearts as he attempts unsuccessfully to fight the battles of his world--both in and out of the newspaper office. His lot is made especially difficult by the taunts and fiendish practical jokes of his boss, Willie Shrike, feature editor of the newspaper; and he slips further and further into a bog of helplessness and immorality as he tries one plan after another to right his course. In the end, he falls victim to a pistol shot fired by Peter Doyle, a cripple who accuses him of raping Mrs. Doyle.

Although the locale and the action of this story are in the newspaper world, the whole picture is scarcely representative. The fact is true that Miss Lonelyhearts is filling a typical function, that of giving advice to readers who have overwhelming problems. The fact is also true that he cracks under the strain of enforced association with Shrike. Yet Miss Lonelyhearts would have faced the same problems in any of a great number of worlds. Certainly he would have met similar problems as a clergyman, a guidance counsellor, a social service worker, or any other person who must discuss personal problems with sufferers. In addition, Willie Shrikes are omnipresent in every occupation; they are not peculiarly indigenous to the newspaper world. In short, Miss Lonelyhearts would have been Miss Lonelyhearts anywhere; he would have failed in any major undertaking because of inadequacies and shortcomings within himself. Hence his problems are self-created rather than the consequence of newspaper journalism.

The unfortunate aftermath of this novel, of course, is that it re-inforces an all too common misconception that all newspapermen must be hardened cynics or they will crack, as Miss Lonelyhearts did, in the whirl of the newspaper business. Many readers have also assumed that Willie Shrike is a typical editor, that newspapermen spend much of their time in pubs, that the newspaper world is one long round of bouts in a dog-eat-dog existence. Also of importance is the fact that nowhere does this novel attempt to interpret the newspaper as an institution. The world of the newspaper is simply a stage or a backdrop against which to move and manipulate a weak and unassertive personality who protests, struggles, and wails before he finally sinks.

A second type of newspaperman to be found in the twentieth century American novel is the character created to fit into a pre-conceived world rather than drawn as a natural part of the world itself or, stated more simply, a character who has been forced into a mold.

The most striking instance of this type appears in the novels of the muckrakers. In these works, the newspapermen have obviously been tailored to the central purpose of the work itself; they harmonize perfectly with the author's clear purpose of villifying the institution of journalism. Examples are the publishers in Upton Sinclair's writings, all of whom are selfish, grasping, egotistical men, and Howard, the newspaper magnate in David Graham Phillip's _The Great God Success_, whose every activity is characterized by lack of principle and concern for his fellowmen.

As one encounters these newspapermen in the muckraking novels, he has a feeling of meeting instruments created for a specific task rather than flesh and blood characters. They are pasteboard figures that form part of a stage setting; they are never people that are likely to be remembered as are Captain Ahab, Christopher Newman, Huck Finn, or even Carol Kennicott.

A slight variation on the character forced into a mold is the one cast as a newspaperman because his activities and philosophy blend into a common conception of the newspaperman; that is to say, the character behaves as a large segment of our population think many or all newspapermen behave. Hence the novelist knowingly or unknowingly encourages this popular notion.

An example is Chick Swallow, the young man around whom the story revolves in Peter De Vries' *Comfort Me With Apples* (1956). Chick leads a life filled with strange and startling experiences. After an unsteady beginning in the workaday world, he drifts into journalism as a columnist for the newspaper in his home town of Decency (note the name), Connecticut. In the course of the story, he carries on an affair with a married woman, moves on the fringe of illegal activities, courts physical danger repeatedly, and lives through a variety of scrapes. Throughout all, he remains the ever-quipping, cocksure young man, both in and out of print.

In casting Chick as a newspaperman, De Vries further gains the opportunity to comment humorously upon many facets of society. As a columnist, Chick can naturally write upon almost any topic that strikes his fancy. Consequently, the novel is filled with puns, jokes, humorous observations and witticisms regarding the citizenry of Decency and life in general. In fact, there are so many attempts at humor that the novel becomes too consciously an attempt to entertain, thereby losing depth of perception in characterization. As a result, Chick never becomes a real person. He remains ever the surface character, relying on a fading humor to ease his way through the world.

The newspaperman who has been created to fit into a pre-conceived world abounds as a minor character in the American novel of the twentieth century. When a novelist needs a somewhat cynical, blunt speaking, uninhibited individual to round out a pre-conceived setting, he often creates his character and then labels him a journalist.

A third type of newspaperman to be found in the twentieth century American novel is the extensively drawn character with a great intensity of purpose. The earliest of such characters is the central figure in Booth Tarkington's _The Gentleman from Indiana_ which first appeared in 1899 but which was revised slightly for a 1902 edition. This story centers about a country newspaper editor and his one-man campaign against political corruption in Carlow County, Indiana. In this novel, Tarkington succeeds rather well in depicting a slowly disappearing species: the crusading editor who has to withstand threats, boycotts, bodily harm, and other pressures in his fight for principles in which he believes.[5]

Tarkington's editor is quite well drawn, although he can scarcely be considered one of the great character creations of American fiction. He appears more as an honest, upright young man who has chanced into the newspaper world to conduct the fight for the improvement of society that he would have engaged in regardless of environment. Nonetheless, he is a fairly convincing depiction of the hard fighting, uncompromising journalist who moves with a strong sense of altruism. This type of editor has now been replaced on the large newspaper by the editorial policy committee. He is still to be found, however, in rural areas and other places where small newspapers exist. There he is likely to be seen battling for better schools, improved sanitation, tighter fiscal procedures, and any other issue which he feels needs support.

There are several other newspapermen in the twentieth century American novel who are drawn as extensively and with as great an intensity of purpose as Tarkington's editor, but most do not succeed so well. Cornelius Tyler, for instance, in Henry Hough Beetle's Lament for a City, begins his professional career on a high plane, only to falter later. Distressed by the changes he sees in his environment, he at first wants desperately to aid in effecting an improvement. Yet he eventually feels the necessity to compromise his ideals--as Tarkington's editor never does--and consequently he is, in part at least, something of a failure.

Gail Wynand in Ayn Rand's The Fountainhead is even less successful as a person and as a high minded journalist. Never one to harbor lofty values, he is coldly factual and cynically attuned to the world about him from the start. He always holds the conviction that the world is a rough, cruel place and one can survive only by facing it with a carefully devised formula based on an unemotional reasoning.

A caution to be noted in considering this category of

the extensively drawn character with great intensity of purpose is this: the character placed herein may sometimes be placed with considerable substance in another category. For example, Howard, the newspaper magnate in David Graham Phillips' The Great God Success, has been placed by this author under the second heading (the character forced into a mold). Yet one can certainly justify any consideration of Howard in the category of the extensively drawn character.

A fourth type of newspaperman found in the American novel of the twentieth century is the one whose professional attributes especially lend themselves to the main purpose of the story. Thus the critical reader gains the impression that the novelist settled on a story or a message first and then chose the newspaper world or a newspaperman as the best means of moving the tale forward. In Laura Z. Hobson's Gentlemen's Agreement (1946), for instance, the primary emphasis is on an examination of the nature of anti-semitism.[6] Philip Green, a new staff writer on a New York newspaper, is given the assignment of learning about anti-semitism in order to write a series of articles on the subject. To accomplish his aim, he poses as a Jew and thereby gains his material first hand.

In casting Green as a newspaperman, Miss Hobson made an adroit move. The reporter on the metropolitan daily maintains a direct contact with all levels of society; and if he is a capable newsman, as Green is, he can always discern the true situation and write of it graphically.

When a main character is as well drawn as Green, the novel has passed a major test. In the instance of this work, however, we have a good but not a great creation.

Other qualities necessary to the great novel, among them the fine "residuum of pleasure" cited by Willa Cather, are missing. Therefore, the novel does not rise far above the commonplace.

(In First Papers (1964), Miss Hobson again employs a newspaperman as a character. This time, however, it is a foreign journalist on American shores. In this novel, two families, one headed by a Russian émigré editor, the other by a staid and upright member of an old New England line of Unitarians, move against the backdrop of the socialist, liberal movement of 1911-20. The editor, however, is presented as a family personality rather than as a newspaperman; and except for occasional observations which reveal his journalistic background, the newspaper as an element never enters the story.)

Another novel which uses a journalist and his professional skills is Helen Mac Innes' The Venetian Affair (1963). In this story, one of the main characters is Bill Fenner, drama critic of the New York Chronicle who, as the story opens, is boarding a plane at Idlewild for a four weeks' vacation-work trip. He is off to Paris to gather material for a series of feature articles on the French national theatre.

On the plane, Fenner meets Albert Goldsmith who, in turn, leads him into a complicated but highly organized international conspiracy. Thereafter the story becomes one long series of thrills, culminating in the near death of Fenner as the enemy is felled by pistol fire in a dark room.

As is true of Miss Hobson, Miss Mac Innes made a sound move in choosing a newspaperman for a main character. Fenner, like the good professional journalist that he is, does not become excited under stress and suspense. His day to day association with the darker side of human character gives him something of an immunity to this kind of strain. Hence he is more capable of remaining calm in the face of great danger. And in this instance, Fenner, as a drama critic, is especially adept at character analysis and knowledgeable in the ways of the intrigue. Therefore, he has another advantage in this situation.

A somewhat less startling use of a newspaperman because of his professional attributes is James Ramsey Ullman's The Sands of Karakorum (1953). In this novel, an American newspaperman presents his first person account of a long journey through Communist China to find two close friends, a missionary and his wife, and afterwards to aid them in their search for the hidden meaning of the mysterious legend about Karakorum, the ancient capital of Genghis Khan.

Obviously, in this work the central character is cast as a newspaperman because of the journalist's ability to cope with such situations as well as his ability to recount them in a direct, readable style.

Many other novelists employ newspapermen as characters in smaller roles because of their talents or professional attributes. Before he commits suicide, the main character in John O'Hara's[7] Appointment in Samarra (1934) holds his last conversation with a young woman society reporter who has come to learn the reason for his canceling a party. Obviously in this instance, a newspaper reporter fills a distinct function in rounding out the story.

The fifth type of newspaperman found in the American

novel of the twentieth century is the one who has been created only to give a variety of occupation to a particular setting. The character fills no special need as a newspaperman: he could serve the main purpose of the story equally well as a toiler in one of many other fields. The author appears to have chosen a newspaperman only to give a dash of the romantic, the worldly, or the heterogeneous to the setting. An example of this type is found in Saul Maloff's _Happy Families_ (1968), a character study of Robert Kalb, an editorial employee of a news magazine, who suffers through a long period of domestic and personal strife before finding a purpose for his life; and in William E. Barrett's _The Edge of Things_ (1960) where a journalist visits an island in the St. Lawrence River to gather material for a book to expose visions (an eight year old girl on the island, Valerie Rivard, has seen a vision). In neither of these novels is a newspaperman, as such, needed. In _Happy Families_, Robert Kalb moves only incidentally in the world of journalism; his problems and his main activities are apart from his work as a newspaperman. In _The Edge of Things_, the visitor could serve the purposes of the novel as effectively as a professional author, a magazine writer, a college professor, or anyone else who writes books.

As is to be expected, however, some difficulty may be encountered in determining whether a given newspaperman character should be classified under the fourth heading (created to fit the main purpose of the story) or the fifth heading (created to give variety). The reason is, of course, that his function as a newspaperman may have some bearing, however remote, on his role in the novel. Two examples can illustrate this point.

In Dan Wickenden's _The Wayfarers_ (1945), the central

figure is the city editor of a midwestern daily whose principal difficulties lie in his private life. Unable to adjust to the death of his wife, he experiences great emotional stress before eventually awakening, too late, to his responsibilities to his children.

There is little of the newspaper world in this novel; the story is concerned almost exclusively with events outside the office. Yet one can argue that the editor, as a working journalist, becomes so involved in other people's worlds that he forgets his own. Hence he is responsible, in part, for his own difficulties. From this deduction, the argument follows that the novelist cast him as an editor to give a ring of veracity to the novel.

In Guard of Honor (1948) James Gould Cozzens recounts a series of episodes occurring within a three-day period in an Air Force base in Florida. A negro lieutenant pilot has violated a regulation involving right-of-way and has received abusive treatment from a white colonel. In subsequent court martial proceedings, Captain Nathaniel Hicks, an editor in civilian life but now an officer in Special Projects, has an opportunity to see justice done. However, he is too busy with his own concerns to make any effort.

Although Cozzens explains that Hicks was an editor in civilian life, he never draws any parallel between his behavior in this incident and his former activity as an editor. Yet once again, some argument can be established for a distant correlation between Hicks the editor and Hicks the military man.

III

In addition to the five classifications discussed above, one can gain an insight into the treatment of the twentieth century American newspaperman in the American novel by examining depictions of men and women who were or still are representative working journalists.

The editor of the small territorial newspaper of the closing years of the last century and the opening years of this century is drawn rather effectively in Edna Ferber's _Cimarron_ (1920). Yancey Cravat, aided by his wife Sabra, controls completely their own little newspaper, _The Oklahoma Wigwam_. He makes all decisions, from the smallest to the most important, without benefit of advice from any quarter. He also evolves an editorial policy squarely in terms of his own viewpoints. The paper "championed the Indians . . . denounced the oil kings . . . laughed at the money grabbers . . . exposed the land thieves . . . was afraid of nothing." Yancey is simply a man of strong convictions, speaking to a reading public as only an editor in his situation could ever do.

The influence which newspaper work with all its day to day pressure, its emphasis on personal acclaim, and its inevitable competition among staff members can have on one's private life is treated in Katherine Brush's _Young Man of Manhattan_ (1930), a lightly written account of a newspaper couple. Toby is a sports writer; Ann, his wife, is a movie columnist. At first their marriage is quite happy; then it deteriorates. The problem, essentially, is that Toby can achieve only moderate success, while Ann reaches newspaper stardom. As a result, Toby becomes jealous and drinks heavily. Ann, meanwhile, develops an excessively confident and overbearing attitude.

Although the story turns principally on marital difficulties, it nonetheless is authentically revelatory of some of the strains which newspaper work can place on a home life. Toby and Ann, like most beginning newspaper writers, are at first quite contented. They have confidence in their own abilities and in their chances for success. Hence their professional life undergirds a satisfactory home life. However, as time passes and one stands still while the other achieves unexpected success, each becomes, in his way, a threat to a continuingly successful marriage. Thus they typify, in some respects at least, the influence which newspaper work can cast on marital tranquility.

The conflict arising because one person cannot adjust to lack of success while the other cannot wear his success with a becoming modesty is an old problem which is not peculiar to the world of journalism: it is to be found in every creative field as well as in the most routine of endeavors. Yet this book is interesting, although certainly far from great, in its insight into this problem as it exists in the domain of the newspaper.

Berry Fleming's Colonel Effingham's Raid (1943) is an entertaining and rather thoroughgoing treatment of a special type of newspaper personality--the writer who suddenly discovers the power of his printed words and proceeds to use that power with a strong and confident sweep. Colonel Effingham, who retired from the army in 1940, returns to his birthplace, a sleepy little Georgia town, and begins to write a weekly column on military affairs for the local paper. After a routine but successful start, he chances to learn of municipal corruption, and true to his military nature, he turns his guns squarely on that which he considers to be of most immediate concern. He fires salvo after salvo, guided only by his firm conviction that he has a mission to accomplish. Nothing can dissuade him from his purpose, despite the magnitude of some of the difficulties encountered.

Colonel Effingham is well drawn, and the story is interestingly told. More important, however, is the focus on a problem related to that handled in Miss Brush's Young Man of Manhattan: it is the unceasing self-appraisal which the newspaper writer with an individual following must conduct to make certain that every judgment has a sound basis in fact; that his power is employed with a measure of proper restraint; and that readers are not being alienated by the overall atmosphere of the presentation.

The scope and importance of this problem of continued self-appraisal can be illustrated by citing some specific errors of judgment in this area. Within the recent past, several nationally syndicated columnists have lost their followings--and their contracts--almost overnight because their opinions offended large segments of readers. A page-one political writer for the New York Times forfeited his stature with his readers and was repudiated editorially by his own paper because of his blind insistence, in the face of overwhelming contradictory evidence, that Cuba's Fidel Castro was a force for good government. A feature writer for a large mid-western paper was deprived of the right to use a by-line because serious inaccuracies in a story aroused a storm of public protest.

Niven Bushch's California Street (1959), which revolves about the life of the central character, Anchylus Saxe, a highly successful, self-made San Francisco publisher, gives a perceptive insight into the home life of a newspaper publisher. The story concerns the attempts of the two younger of Saxe's three daughters to obtain from him the power of proxy. With this power, they hope to wrest control of his newspapers, destroy him personally, and exclude his eldest daughter (who is only their half-sister because of her illegitimate birth) from any share of the wealth.

Amidst the intrigue, complexities, and maneuvering which result, the plot becomes highly involved and, at times, melodramatic. In the scenes involving journalism, however, the book is strong, especially as it reveals the private mind of the newspaper owner. Saxe, in fact, is so much the true newspaperman that he allows his gossip columnist to deride a member of his own family simply because of his newspaperman's belief that no one must be shielded from the public eye.

John Gunther's The Lost City (1964) creates an authentic and perceptive view of the life of the American newspaper correspondent in a European country. This novel, based on Gunther's own experience as a correspondent in Vienna in the early 1930's,[8] turns on the life of a husband and wife, Mason and Paula Jarrett, as they move in their circle of American newspapermen and those from other countries. The group, which meets almost nightly in a coffee house, is shown as it converses, philosophizes, and passes judgment on a variety of subjects ranging from small talk to matters of pressing international import.

Although the story concerns itself principally with the marital difficulties of the Jarretts, it also gives an excellent panorama of the foreign correspondent and his particular kind of work. Usually, this type of newspaperman is highly intelligent; he is genuinely skilled in the interpretation of the political and other events about him; and he has a strong sense of the importance of his work. In most instances, he is an exceptionally capable newsman who has been advanced to this important position through demonstrated ability.

This novel also throws light on the manner in which the American foreign correspondent often evaluates the activities of his own country. Mason Jarrett and his fellow American newspapermen have an unquestioned loyalty to the United States. But they are also clearly alarmed about official Washington's failure to discern the threat of an ever-expanding Hitlerism. Hence they pass judgments that are surprising in both their detached objectivity and their obviously prejudiced element.

Because Gunther has always striven to enhance his reputation as an authentic journalist and a careful writer of history, he has taken great pains with this novel. The result is a readable and revelatory work.

The consequences to which the American newspaper correspondent who runs afoul of a foreign government may be exposed are treated in Paul Gallico's Trial by Terror (1959). In this novel the central character is making an independent investigation of several cases of foreigners who have been seized, charged with trumped-up allegations, and punished. In the process, the correspondent is imprisoned and brainwashed to the extent that he, too, is prepared to "confess." Only through the alertness of friends is he saved.

Although this novel tends to be highly dramatic and, at times overly pat in its formula, it nonetheless treats effectively a common situation--the situation where the American foreign correspondent, through naiveté or conviction, employs a tenet of American editorial policy in a nation where that tenet is certain to spell trouble. In the United States no self-respecting newspaperman would think twice about his right to investigate and print the facts of an injustice. In a non-democratic nation, however, that same newspaperman would have to conduct himself in an entirely different manner. Hence this novel presents a typical American newspaperman in a typical situation.

Still another facet of the life of the American foreign correspondent is handled in Robert Nathan's A Star in the Wind (1962). This novel revolves about the activities and thoughts of Joseph Victor, an American correspondent assigned to cover the Arab-Israel War that resulted in the creation of the new Jewish state. Victor, because of his Jewish background and his sensitive nature, becomes deeply and emotionally involved in every phase of the conflict. From his conversations and observations comes a perceptive revelation of the reaction which a journalist may feel to the "news" which he is covering.

This novel is also quite effective in depicting the day-to-day stress under which many newspapermen must work as well as being another refutation of the all too popular judgment that all journalists are hardened cynics, completely immune to any kind of emotional strain.

Thomas W. Duncan's Gus the Great (1959) is the story

of Augustus H. Burgoyne, who has been variously a showman, a promoter, and a newspaperman--always with great ambitions and great aims but never achieving anything approaching a commensurate success. Gus' tragedy, basically, is that he seems unable to realize that he has failed, and he does not profit from his experiences.

In creating Gus, Burgoyne has depicted a type to be found in every city room (as well, of course, as in many other places). He is the dreamer who wants big things, who never obtains them, but who continues to dream and talk and dream and talk. This type is usually held by his fellow journalists in a kind of limited affection mixed with pleasant contempt and pity. He is generally given only the most routine of assignments, and he is rarely placed in any position demanding initiative or sound judgment.

In Mrs. Daffodil (1957), Gladys Taber presents an interesting picture of a woman newspaper columnist at home. The main character, Mrs. Daffodil, lives in the Connecticut countryside with her friend Kate, and here she unfolds her ideas, garbed in a homespun philosophy, on a wide variety of subjects.

Although this novel is, for the most part, a routine production, it does cast a clear light on the manner in which such a columnist as Mrs. Daffodil gathers and cogitates upon her material. It also explains rather clearly the appeal which this kind of material may exert.

Ben Ames Williams' Splendor (1927) tells the story of a very common type of newspaperman who receives little or no attention in fiction. This is the man of limited ability who performs routine and unspectacular duties for a professional lifetime. Henry begins his career as a copy boy, rises through seniority to cover ordinary events, but then falls back into a drab position where he is all but forgotten. Meanwhile, the author parallels his character's newspaper life with his home life across the fifty-year period covered by the story.

The significance of this novel is simply that it treats Henry as representative of a numerous species. Hence it focuses attention on the fact that the newspaper world has its share of run-of-the-mill people as judged from the standpoints of ability, services performed, and color.

Notes

1. New Yorker, January 5, 1952.

2. The New York Times editorial group meets in a room that could just as well serve for a large business house. There are the usual conference table, chairs, and other furniture found in the business corporation; and the room has maps, books, and records readily available for the conferees.

3. Witla is the most familiar example because this Dreiser novel has been more widely read than any other twentieth century American novel employing this type of character.

4. Reprinted in 1966 with noisy publicity about its being the "classic" novel regarding newspaper journalism. To this author, the wide reception accorded this novel has always been a matter of surprise. It is not well written; it becomes, on occasions, downright maudlin; and it fails in any attempt to create convincing characters. Nonetheless, it has been widely read and praised by many competent newspapermen, and it appears on the reading list for journalism majors in many universities.

5. The most celebrated real-life editor of this kind was Elijah P. Lovejoy whose stand for abolition led to his death at the hands of an angry mob on November 7, 1837, in Alton, Illinois. Lovejoy was setting up a fourth press after three others had been thrown into a nearby river.

6. An interesting comparison can be made with Saul Bellow's The Victim (1947) which also treats the subject of anti-semitism.

7. John O'Hara shows an excellent grasp and understanding of the working reporter in a short story entitled "Claude Emerson, Reporter," which appears as one of twenty-three selections in his volume, Cape Cod Lighter (1963). Emerson is depicted in the light of the settled conviction of many old time journalists that newspapermen are born, not made. Emerson displays all the attributes of the best of reporters. He can sense the presence of news; he can place his finger unerringly on the important facts of the story; and he can write in a style that delights the readers of the small town paper for which he works. With all these attributes, he has a further requisite for success: he has built up a solid rapport with citizens of all levels, thereby gaining an exclusive avenue to many stories that are news for his paper. Above all, he is a true newspaperman in every sense of the term. He feels that he is exactly where he belongs; he proceeds with a remarkable deftness in every phase of his work; and he is always convinced of the all-pervading significance of newspaper journalism.

8. In an "Author's Note" to this novel, Gunther wants the fact understood that the book is a novel. He says that he has "taken several liberties" with facts, but that the work is "not reminiscence or disguised autobiography."

Chapter 6

Conclusion

I

As one views the treatment of the twentieth century American newspaper in the American novel, he can discern several important facts. Most noticeable, there is an absence of any thorough consideration of the newspaper as an institution; that is to say, nowhere can one find the all-pervasive examination, the deliberate and capable reflection, and the careful analysis which other major institutions within our society have received. Many novelists have handled quite competently various facets of the newspaper world, and several have drawn authentic and convincing newspapermen; but none has produced an extensive interpretation of the total institution of the twentieth century American newspaper.

Naturally, no single thesis can account for this lack of extensive consideration. Neither can one delineate the total situation within a few sentences. Considerable light, nonetheless, can be cast by considering the principal reasons. The most obvious reason is that no major novelist has made the attempt. Critics can agree that only writers meriting the accolade of "genuine artist" are capable of perceptive, definitive interpretations; and in twentieth century America, no novelist of this caliber ever focused his prolonged attention on journalism. Those generally considered to be of front-rank stature--Mark Twain, Henry James, Willa Cather, Edith

Wharton, William Faulkner--have either been concerned with other fields, or they have touched journalism only lightly. The same has been true of those immediately below the top level--for example, Theodore Dreiser, William Dean Howells, Hamlin Garland--and it has been true of lesser writers with wide followings--for instance, Sinclair Lewis, James T. Farrell, and John Dos Passos.

A second important reason is interests. Novelists, like performers in other creative fields, gravitate naturally toward subjects and topics with which they feel an affinity. If they are interested primarily in creating people, as Willa Cather and Thomas Wolfe were, they have little cause to treat institutions. If they are interested in specific types of people in specific milieux, as Ellen Glasgow and William Faulkner were, they handle institutions only as they touch the lives of those people in those settings. But if they are committed to a criticism of their times, as Garland and Lewis were, and Dos Passos is, they are likely to consider, among other things, the institutions about them. However, the capable novelists in this last named category have not reacted, as this book attempts to demonstrate, according to expectation; that is to say, they have not reacted by considering the institution of the newspaper in America.

The matter of interests poses another question: since so many American novelists knew the newspaper through first-hand contact as working journalists, why did not more write of it? Certainly writers like Dreiser, Lewis, Farrell, and Dos Passos must have reflected on the final significance of journalism in American life as a result of their careers on newspapers. Yet they either treated the newspaper lightly or not at all. One also wonders why these same novelists did not draw more on the many interesting personalities which one encounters in the newspaper world.

A third reason for the absence of any extensive interpretation of newspaper journalism in the twentieth century American novel lies in the novelist's conception of the role of the novel. Every literary artist naturally views the various media of expression--i.e., the novel, the essay, the poem, the drama, the short story--as the vehicles for handling specific types of subjects. Consequently, some novelists believe that such a subject as journalism can be treated more effectively in forms other than the novel.

William Dean Howells, for example, presents his insights into journalism in essay form. James Thurber reflects on the newspaper and its functions in his autobiographical works. Mark Twain and John O'Hara employ the short story for the same purpose. Hence in each instance one finds an interest and an interpretation of one or more phases of journalism cast in a form other than the novel, even though each author is a capable novelist.

II

American novelists have not placed an equal emphasis on the major questions raised by the twentieth century American newspaper. Some questions they have treated rather extensively; some they have treated only partially; and others they have ignored entirely.

The major questions treated rather extensively are yellow journalism, the dangers of the unrestrained columnists, and the threats of the powerful executive.

Yellow journalism, which made its strongest bid in the early decades of the current century, has occasioned many novels dealing with the evils found therein. Yet no one of these novels, despite the extent of its treatment, represents a genuinely competent evaluation. Novelists like Miriam Michelson tend to over-emphasize the condition; novelists like David Grayson tend to over-simplify it; and novelists like Henry S. Harrison tend to view it from a distorted perspective. Seemingly no novelist displays the insight into the problem necessary for proper examination and analysis.

The dangers of the unrestrained columnist are touched upon clearly in several novels but are treated extensively in Emile Henry Gauvreau's _The Scandal Monger,_ an obvious examination of the role and influence of Walter Winchell. Gauvreau tends at times to condemn overly strongly; yet he does present clearly the perils involved.

The threats of the powerful executive are handled in a variety of manners. William R. Hereford's _The Demagog_ shows the dangers of chain ownership in the hands of a man like William Randolph Hearst. Robert Herrick's _The Great God Success,_ beneath its muckraking atmosphere, delineates the flagrant power which an individual publisher can wield. And Ayn Rand's _The Fountainhead,_ despite a certain superficiality of treatment, exhibits the inherent dangers of a distorted personality serving as a newspaper executive. Meanwhile, there are novels which show how influential an editor or a publisher may be in community and other affairs.

The major questions which are treated only partially are quite numerous. Theodore Dreiser in _An American_

Tragedy handles the underlying danger of satisfying an emotional and uninformed public at the expense of objectivity. Clarence B. Kelland in Contraband portrays rather well the obligation of a newspaper to contribute to the uplift of society. Joseph A. Altsheler's Guthrie of the Times, its weaknesses notwithstanding, depicts the function of the newspaper as a crusading force. Richard Powell's Daily and Sunday considers the adjustments of the newspaper to the society in which it exists. These novels are cited, of course, merely as examples. There are many other treatments of these and other questions. Yet no one of these novels examines its subject fully. It merely treats a part of the total problem.

The questions which have been ignored--or touched so lightly as to be almost meaningless--represent some of the most important issues of the period. They are (1) the threats to freedom of expression raised by the Federal Government and the bar associations; (2) censorship implications of United States Supreme Court decisions; (3) the actual decrease in number of newspapers with the concurrent rise of "one newspaper" cities; (4) the increasing control of the media of mass communications by fewer and fewer persons; and (5) the loss of opportunity for a man of limited financial means to launch a newspaper.

III

The influence of newspaper work on the person engaged therein has always been an interesting and elusive matter. There can be little doubt that the working journalist, who day after day meets the illicit, the immoral, the dramatic, and the many other situations that make "news," feels a distinct type of effect. He experiences a peculiarly individual influence akin to that cast on the police by their constant handling of lawbreakers, that thrown on judges by their daily associations with persons in deep troubles, and that exerted on surgeons by their inevitable handling of human life in critical situations.

Several of the novelists discussed in these pages have treated aspects of this influence quite capably. Gene Fowler, Robert Nathan, Henry Hough Beetle, and John Gunther, for example, have drawn convincing pictures of specific pressures on working newspapermen; and Thomas Wolfe, Ayn Rand, Charles Angoff, and Niven Busch have presented vivid depictions of individual reactions to phases of newspaper work. Yet no American novelist within this sixty-nine year period has created a genuinely memorable newspaperman character; that is to say, none has given to American fiction an immortal personality in the mold of Mark Twain's Huck Finn or Henry James' Christopher Newman. Thus one can safely state that no American novelist has portrayed in the manner of the master painter all the dominant qualities of the American "newspaperman."

Furthermore, in creating newspapermen characters, the American novelist has tended to err in the direction of popular misconceptions. He has tended to employ misfits, maladjusted personalities, and moral degenerates rather than wholesome, well rounded people. Hence he has aided essentially in strengthening these popular conclucions.

IV

As one considers all the pertinent facts regarding the treatment of the American newspaper from 1900 to 1969 in the

American novel, he finds that he must agree with the sarcasm-tinged statement so often made by book reviewers passing judgment on a novel about things journalistic: the great American newspaper novel still remains to be written.

Index